Don

W9-CDS-428

THE MORTGAGE MANUAL

THE MORTGAGE MANUAL

The Complete Guide to Choosing the Real Estate Loan That's Best for You

Don DeBat

Edited by Thomas A. Kelly

CONTEMPORARY
BOOKS, INC.
CHICAGO ■ NEW YORK

Library of Congress Cataloging-in-Publication Data

DeBat, Don.
   The mortgage manual.

   1. Mortgage loans—United States.   2. House buying—
United States.   I. Title.
HG2040.5.U5D423   1986   332.7'22   86-23972
ISBN 0-8092-4890-5 (pbk.)

Published by Contemporary Books, Inc.
180 North Michigan Avenue, Chicago, Illinois 60601
Manufactured in the United States of America
Library of Congress Catalog Card Number: 86-23972
International Standard Book Number: 0-8092-4890-5

Published simultaneously in Canada by Beaverbooks, Ltd.
195 Allstate Parkway, Valleywood Business Park
Markham, Ontario L3R 4T8 Canada

*To my children, Aimée and Erik,
and a very special lady,
for all the weekends lost*

CONTENTS

ACKNOWLEDGMENTS

Some of the material in this book was researched and written while the author gathered information for his weekly real estate column published in the *Chicago Sun-Times*.

This book would not have been possible without the cooperation and assistance of many individuals and organizations. Thomas A. Kelly, features copy desk chief of the *Sun-Times*, skillfully edited the manuscript and provided many organizational ideas.

Thanks is also due to my bosses: *Sun-Times* president and publisher Robert E. Page, managing editor Kenneth D. Towers, and assistant managing editor for features Scott Powers, who encouraged me to take time off from a busy schedule to complete this project.

Also, real estate lawyer Marshall J. Moltz, partner in the firm of Randall, Gayle, Patt & Moltz; mortgage analyst Gary S. Meyers, president of Gary S. Meyers & Associates; David Podbelski, chief of mortgage credit at the Chicago office of the Department of Housing and

Urban Development; Michael L. Allen, president of Crown Mortgage Co.; and Maurice Sanderman, president of Sundance Homes.

In addition, the United States League of Savings Institutions, the Mortgage Bankers Association of America, the National Association of Home Builders, The National Association of Realtors, the Federal National Mortgage Association, and the Family Backed Mortgage Association.

THE MORTGAGE MANUAL

CHAPTER 1

A SURVIVAL COURSE IN BIG-LOAN HUNTING

Before venturing into the uncharted territory of today's mortgage market, home buyers need to pass a consumer survival course in big-loan hunting.

Whether you are shopping for your first home, moving up to a bigger house, or hunting for a retirement residence, cutting a path through the Mortgage-land jungle can be financially perilous for the unwary.

Home-loan interest rates in 1986 dipped to the lowest level in seven years, and that was good news for all buyers. However, rising housing prices have partially offset the rate decrease. Many young people still find it a challenge to save a large enough down payment and to qualify for a mortgage.

In 1949, the average homeowner spent 14 percent of his earnings on mortgage payments. Today, it takes at least 28 percent of the average homeowner's gross income just to meet the monthly mortgage payment and pay real estate taxes and insurance. Two of every three first-time buyers need two incomes to make the mortgage payments.

In 1982, when home loan rates averaged about 15 percent, buyers needed an annual income of $44,743 to qualify for a $72,000, fixed-rate, 30-year loan. The monthly payments for principal and interest would have been $911.

Mortgage Payments and Income Needed to Buy an $80,000 Home

Use the following chart to estimate how much income you need to qualify for the monthly payments necessary to buy an $80,000 home. The numbers assume a 10 percent down payment of $8,000 and monthly principal and interest (P&I) payments on a $72,000 mortgage for 30 years. Annual taxes and homeowners' insurance payments (T&I) are estimated at 2 percent of the purchase price, or $1,600. For simplicity, private mortgage insurance is ignored. The total monthly payment for principal, interest, taxes, and insurance (PITI) is exactly 28 percent of the minimum qualifying monthly income.

Interest rate	Monthly P&I	Monthly T&I	Total PITI	Annual income to qualify
8%	$528	$133	$661	$28,329
9	580	133	713	30,557
10	632	133	765	32,786
11	686	133	819	35,100
12	741	133	874	37,457
13	797	133	930	39,857
14	853	133	986	42,257
15	911	133	1,044	44,743

However, the sharp rate decreases of 1985 and 1986 opened a window of opportunity for home buyers. A buyer who grabbed a 9 percent mortgage qualified for a $72,000 loan with income of only $30,557. Monthly principal and interest payments dropped to an affordable $580 a month—a 37 percent difference from payments on a 15 percent loan.

IS HOME OWNERSHIP WANING?

Rising home prices and the historically high interest rates of the early 1980s caused the rate of home ownership in the United States to level off—even drop—for the first time since the Great Depression.

After steadily increasing since the 1930s, home ownership peaked in the third quarter of 1980 when 65.8 percent of the nation's residents owned their home, according to the U.S. Bureau of the Census. In 1985, only 63.9 percent of Americans—a decrease of more than a million households—owned their own home.

This trend has been most apparent among young households, especially those headed by persons under 35 years of age. In 1981, 43.3 percent of the Americans in this age group owned their own home. In the first quarter of 1986, the figure was 39.7 percent, the census bureau reports.

But if you're among the third of Americans who don't own a home, don't despair. It still is possible to buy, now that rates are way down on their continuing roller coaster ride.

THE HOMEOWNING MAJORITY

If you are old enough to remember World War II, radio thrillers, and the Brooklyn Dodgers, you've probably long forgotten the worry of saving for a down payment and applying for a mortgage on your first home.

Even if you bought your home in the era of 5 percent fixed-rate mortgages, lend an ear. The rules of the mortgage game have changed and continue to change. Someday soon you may want to swap that 1950s ranch in suburbia for a retirement condo in Florida, and then you'll understand why so many young buyers look so bewildered.

A few years ago, taking out a home loan was as easy as a Sunday stroll at the zoo. By merely visiting the local bank or savings and loan association, filling out an application, and passing a credit check, borrowers were well on their way to owning the American Dream.

However, you can't use yesterday's assumptions in today's mortgage market. Today, all borrowers—young, old, and in between—must educate themselves so they can track down a mortgage that meets their needs. This book will introduce you to the most popular types of home loans now available and explain how they work.

While most buyers today are applying for old-fashioned fixed-rate mortgages, the plain vanilla variety of home loan, don't make up your mind until you have studied all the options.

OLD-FASHIONED MORTGAGES

Conventional fixed-rate mortgages feature an interest rate and monthly payment that do not change over the course of the loan, usually 15 or 30 years. A new twist offered by some lenders allows payments every other week, which means you can pay off the loan faster, saving thousands of dollars in interest.

The typical fixed-rate mortgage is set up so that the interest portion of each monthly payment decreases over time, while the principal portion increases. The total payment each month stays the same.

Another fixed-rate loan possibility is the government-backed mortgage. Home loans backed by the Federal Housing Administration and Veterans Administration are much like conventional fixed-rate loans. FHA and VA loans, however, allow lower down payments and can be assumed by the next owner of the home. The trade-off may be in government red tape and lengthy processing time. Also, these loans often require more fees at closing than conventional fixed-rate mortgages.

In 1986, the heavy demand for such loans has caused funding problems. Both the FHA and VA ordered lenders to stop taking or processing applications because the agencies had reached their credit ceilings. Congress eventually raised the limits, putting the agencies back in business.

NEW BREED OF HOME LOANS

Whether you are a first-time buyer or a seasoned homeowner looking for a retirement home, there are many new types of mortgages that you may want to study. Unfortunately, these loans often complicate the rules of the mortgage game.

For example, in the early 1980s, thousands of borrowers in the United States took adjustable-rate mortgages (ARMs), but experts say many of them don't understand how the payment or rate adjustments are made.

Basically, an ARM is a loan with an interest rate that can change as often as specified. Some may change every six months, some every year or five years. Interest rate adjustments are tied to some financial index—the rate on one-year U.S. Treasury bills, for instance. If the rates on T-bills go up, so does the rate on your mortgage. On some ARMs, this may affect your monthly payment. On others it may affect the length of the mortgage or your equity in the home.

For young buyers who have low current income but high earning potential, there are other innovative financing options. For example, payments on growing-equity mortgages (GEMs) and graduated-payment mortgages (GPMs) are designed to increase with the borrower's income.

Older homeowners can take out a mortgage without buying a home. That's because a reverse-equity mortgage converts the equity in their homes into cash.

Balloon loans and buying on contract aren't popular when mortgage rates are affordable, but these loan options thrive when interest charges are high.

Clearly, all these options make the unsophisticated borrower easy prey for the creatures that prowl Mortgageland. The jungle path to home ownership is no Sunday stroll, but this book should help borrowers cut their way through the complicated choices, see-sawing interest rates, special fees, and processing delays.

CHAPTER 2

SOURCES OF MORTGAGE MONEY

Until a few years ago, more than half the money for America's home loans came from savers' deposits in savings and loan associations (S&Ls), mutual savings banks, and other thrift institutions.

Today, however, savings institutions' mortgages often are sold to investors. And giant mortgage companies have staked claims to a substantial share of the market. This, too, has changed how home buyers go about getting a mortgage.

Through the mid- to late 1970s, S&Ls paid low interest rates on their large, insured savings deposits, and many states regulated the maximum interest rate that could be charged on a home loan. Maximum rates paid to savers also were regulated by states or the federal government, so thrift institutions had the cheapest money to lend and were the most active in financing private homes.

Federal tax regulations are structured to encourage thrifts to invest at least 80 percent of their assets in mortgages for residences.

However, in the early 1980s, the arrival of volatile interest rates and the deregulation of financial institutions turned the home-loan market upside down.

As regulations on savings and lending were phased out, depositors shopped around for the best return on their savings, often moving their money out of the thrift institutions. With less inexpensive money to lend, the lenders turned increasingly to capital markets for funds with which to make mortgages.

START AT AN S&L

Despite market changes, your local S&Ls still are a good place to start your search for a home loan. These institutions still specialize in long-term mortgages within their service area.

Generally, S&Ls are more sensitive to borrowers' needs because they want to service the loans and maintain a good customer relationship. However, you may pay a slightly higher rate at an S&L, because few of them handle the volume of business that industry leaders and mortgage firms accommodate.

When the mortgage market is booming, a borrower who deals with an S&L may have his or her loan processed and approved faster than at a mortgage company. Often appraisers and credit and survey companies try to get a major S&L's work done as quickly as possible, because the thrift institution sends them so much business. Mortgage companies may handle more loans, but they often are spread throughout the country, not just in one city or county.

Most S&Ls will lend up to 95 percent of a home's appraised value, so qualified borrowers can get a mortgage with as little as 5 percent down. S&Ls often give preferential treatment to borrowers who have accounts with them already.

S&Ls offer a wide variety of financing plans, but to protect themselves against inflation, many institutions encourage home buyers to choose adjustable-rate mortgages. Because this type of loan allows lenders to raise rates when inflation increases, S&Ls usually offer ARMs at initial rates about two percentage points below a comparable fixed-rate loan.

If the thrift institution is federally chartered and regulated by the Federal Home Loan Bank Board, it can offer all federally approved loan plans, including ARMs and graduated-payment mortgages. State-chartered S&Ls also offer a wide assortment of mortgages. However, many states prohibit thrifts from making loans that call for negative amortization—adding interest to your principal, thus eating into your equity.

Although thrift institutions hold billions of dollars of mortgages in their portfolios, they have increasingly sold loans into the secondary mortgage market.

By using secondary market organizations such as the Federal Home Loan Mortgage Corporation as a conduit, S&Ls sell fixed-rate loans to investors, thus reducing the potential for being stuck with old 11 percent loans, for example, when other lenders are charging 13 or 14 percent.

Though this practice may seem to have little impact on borrowers—who continue to send monthly payments to the lender—it does allow lenders to make more loans than otherwise possible. A more detailed discussion of the secondary market can be found later in this chapter.

COMMERCIAL BANKS

Second to savings and loan associations in total investment in home mortgages, commercial banks actually concentrate most of their efforts in serving business clients. Most of the funds in such a bank come from short-term checking and savings accounts, and much of its mortgage activity involves loans for offices and business and construction loans.

But much as some appliance dealers specialize in microwaves, while others rely on washers and dryers, some banks take a more active role in residential mortgages. Banks generally are permitted to lend up to 75 percent of the value of the property. That means you'll need a 25 percent down payment to qualify. Don't expect to find great bargains at most commercial banks, because their mortgage rates usually are on a par with or even slightly higher than those at S&Ls. But it never hurts to compare rates.

MORTGAGE BANKERS AND BROKERS

If you obtain a home loan from a mortgage banking company, the firm probably will sell your loan to an investor and use the proceeds to make new loans. But the company will continue to collect your monthly payments and service your loan. Unlike an S&L, however, the mortgage company probably is not based in your town or even in your state.

Mortgage banking companies make their money on loan origination fees and any profit they can make from selling the loans in the secondary market to institutional investors, such as life insurance companies or pension funds.

These aggressive loan brokers will make conventional residential mortgages, and some firms specialize in FHA and VA loans because these secure, government-backed mortgages are easy to sell to investors. Today, mortgage bankers originate 80 percent of all government-insured home loans.

Often, mortgage companies offer the most competitive rates in town, because they deal almost directly with investors. But these lenders often charge higher points than S&Ls.

During the hot real estate market of 1986, mortgage bankers and brokers came under heavy criticism in some states because of processing delays, which caused interest-rate commitments to expire before loans were closed. Thousands of consumers paid hundreds of dollars each to "lock in" rates early in 1986 and then ended up paying higher rates and more points because interest charges had increased since they had applied. The protection of locked-in rates was a mirage once the rate commitment had expired.

Mortgage companies said single-digit interest rates created a stampede that buried appraisal, survey, and credit companies in an avalanche of work. There was nothing they could do, the firms said, although some offered to cancel loan applications, refund fees not yet spent, and turn over completed credit report, survey, and appraisal papers to the borrowers.

Although S&Ls also experienced delays, many institutions honored their expired commitments because they wanted to maintain good customer relationships. S&Ls had more flexibility than mortgage firms because at least some of their loans are made with savers' deposits.

Mortgage brokers and bankers were caught in a squeeze because their loans already were sold to investors. When rate commitments expired and interest rates moved higher, mortgage companies could pass the new market rate on to borrowers or take a loss on the loans.

CREDIT UNIONS AND PENSION FUNDS

Home buyers who belong to one of the nation's 22,000 federal- and state-regulated U.S. credit unions soon may have a new source of mortgage money.

Credit unions with less than $2 million in assets may write residential mortgages without prior approval from the National Credit Union Administration. In the past, credit unions have specialized in short-term consumer loans for their more than 44 million members.

Pension funds are loaded with cash that could be used for mortgages. For example, the AFL-CIO union pension fund holds $50 billion of the nation's $80 to $90 billion total assets in multi-employer pension plans.

Because pension funds seek a secure, fixed rate of return for their participants, mortgages may be an ideal investment for them. Recently, the U.S. Labor Department gave limited approval for pension plans to offer their participants residential mortgages at below prevailing rates. Because of regulation changes, pension funds soon could become like mortgage companies and fund home loans.

THE SECONDARY MARKET

The secondary market, which links lenders to capital markets, is the fastest growing segment of the home mortgage business.

This dramatic growth is not apparent to the average borrower, who may never realize his or her mortgage was sold by an S&L, bank, or mortgage company. The homeowner whose mortgage is sold through the secondary market continues to make monthly payments to the original lender, which services the loan for the investor.

In its early development, the secondary market helped financial institutions shift funds from regions of the country where there was extra mortgage money to areas where available cash couldn't meet demand.

As the secondary market developed over the past decade, it has become an important mechanism for increasing the flow of funds from Wall Street's bond markets to Main Street's mortgage needs. In doing so, it helped develop standardized mortgage instruments.

A number of players make up the secondary market.

These include the Federal National Mortgage Association, the Government National Mortgage Association, and the Federal Home Loan Mortgage Corporation.

Established by Congress to buy FHA loans in 1938 when credit was scarce, FNMA (Fannie Mae) is the largest single investor in residential mortgages. It became a private, for-profit corporation in 1968 and began buying conventional loans in 1970. Acting like a giant savings and loan association, Fannie Mae buys mortgages from lenders and packages them into securities for investors.

The Government National Mortgage Association (GNMA, or Ginnie Mae) was established as an arm of the U.S. Department of Housing and Urban Development in 1968 to provide secondary-market support for the government's housing programs. It buys FHA and VA mortgages, pools them into securities, and then sells them to investors.

The Federal Home Loan Mortgage Corporation (FHLMC, nicknamed Freddie Mac) was established in 1970 to provide a secondary market for conventional loans. All of its stock is owned by the Federal Home Loan Bank system and much of its business is with savings and loans. Freddie Mac packages its loans in pools and sells participation certificates to investors.

In addition to these major secondary market corporations and associations, home loans also are sold by mortgage brokers to S&Ls, insurance companies, pension funds, and other investors.

So, whether it's an S&L, bank, mortgage company, credit union or pension fund, today's home buyer has a potpourri of mortgage sources from which to choose. With the help of more standardized mortgage instruments and the tremendous liquidity created by the secondary mortgage market, even novice home-loan hunters should be able to find the funding they need.

CHAPTER 3

INTEREST RATES: WHY ARE THEY SO VOLATILE?

Everything has a price, and a mortgage is no exception. The interest rate—or price—of a home loan is determined in the marketplace, where money is borrowed and lent

In early 1986, fixed rates on long-term mortgages dropped below 10 percent for the first time in the 1980s, creating a boom of home sales and a stampede of refinancing activity. Although rates climbed back to 10 to 10.5 percent in mid-1986, many experts expect them to decline again.

To understand the roller coaster nature of home-loan rates, you have to look back over five or six decades. Mortgage rates have come a long way since the 1920s, when home buyers were required to make 50 percent down payments and finance the balance with a balloon loan that was due in full—or could be refinanced—after five years.

When many of the balloon loans came due during the Great Depression of the 1930s, millions of borrowers couldn't afford to pay them off. They lost their homes.

In 1934, Congress created the Federal Housing Administration to encourage home ownership in the United States. The FHA created the first government-backed long-term home loans that could be paid off in affordable monthly installments.

In those days, lenders charged 3 percent to 4 percent annual interest on home loans. It wasn't until inflation started to heat up in the 1950s that all interest rates, including those on mortgages, began their gradual climb. By the early 1960s, lenders were charging 6 percent on 30-year fixed-rate mortgages.

THE TIGHT-MONEY ERA

Mortgage rates began to increase faster in the early 1970s. At the beginning of the decade, mortgage rates were in the range of 7 percent to 8 percent. A recession, the oil crisis, and the tight-money period of 1973–74 sent rates up to 9 percent. During the housing boom years of 1975–78, rates again stabilized at a new plateau in the 8 percent to 9 percent range.

At the beginning of the 1980s, deregulation of the banking industry prompted many substantial changes. Limits were lifted on interest rates that lenders could offer to depositors. State laws that limited the rates lenders could charge for loans were wiped off the books. As mentioned earlier, mortgage lenders now could compete for funds with commercial banks, businesses, and the federal government.

Unfortunately, deregulation, soaring inflation, and the recession of 1980 coincided to send an interest-rate tremor stronger than the eruption of Mount St. Helens through the home finance market.

Record high interest rates of nearly 20 percent resulted from inflationary pressures generated in the

American economy through "two decades of reckless spending by Congress and the attempt of our government to try to penalize the industrious and reward the indolent," said Merrill Butler, 1980 president of the National Association of Home Builders.

When inflation was running at 9 and 10 percent, Butler said, "It doesn't make any difference whether mortgage rates are 15 percent or 18 percent—you can only kill a man once. And we were killed off when rates started going above 13 percent."

In Illinois, one of the states hit hardest by the housing recession, mortgage rates hit a record 17.5 percent in spring of 1980. In New York and California, home loan rates peaked in the 17 percent to 18 percent range.

By summer 1980, the crunch eased and mortgages were available at about 11.5 percent to 12 percent in most sections of the nation. But by year's end, rates bounced back to the 14 percent to 16 percent range.

At 16 percent interest—the prevailing rate nationwide at the end of 1980—only 4 out of every 100 families in America could afford to carry a $60,000 mortgage for 30 years.

Mortgage lending was down to a trickle. Several of Chicago's top savings and loan associations reported hefty losses in 1980, and a third of the home builders in the area left the business.

The skyrocketing rates and deregulation also spurred use of the adjustable-rate mortgage. ARMs allow lenders to increase or decrease the interest rate—and usually a borrower's monthly payment—based on the movement of previously agreed-upon indexes.

After deregulation, lenders declared that the fixed-rate, long-term mortgage was dead. They said the volatile marketplace made it impossible for them to lock in rates for 20 or 30 years. Instead, they said, mortgage rates would have to vary with economic conditions. They warned that S&Ls couldn't stay in business long with their money lent out on 8 percent mortgages for 20 more years and current savers being paid 12 percent on certificates of deposit.

Soon afterward, economists and lenders said the single-digit mortgage was dead. Forecasters said mortgage rates of 9 percent would never be seen again in our lifetime. Their crystal balls must have been clouded by their own short-sightedness.

History of Fixed-Rate Mortgage Interest

Here is a list of long-term effective interest rates charged by savings institutions over the years for conventional loans on new homes. This chart was compiled by the U.S. League of Savings Institutions from figures gathered by the Federal Home Loan Bank Board.

Year	Rate
1965	5.81%
1970	8.45
1971	7.74
1972	7.60
1973	7.96
1974	8.92
1975	9.00
1976	9.00
1977	9.02
1978	9.56
1979	10.78
1980	12.66
1981	14.70
1982	15.14
1983	12.66
1984	12.37
1985	11.58

REBIRTH OF FIXED-RATE LOANS

In the recovery years of 1983 and 1984, charges on fixed-rate mortgages gradually declined to 12 to 14 percent. (See the chart on page 17.) By 1985, fixed-rate mortgages were available at 11 percent. A wide variety of ARM loans at *initial* discounted rates of 8 to 10 percent also were available.

Deeply discounted single-digit ARMs enjoyed a brief popularity in 1983–85. At one point, lenders boasted that ARMs accounted for half their new loan business. Consumers didn't fare too badly either. With an initial rate of 10 percent, for example, a borrower was paying perhaps 3 percentage points less than a fixed-rate loan would require. The only risk was that rates might increase.

But by late 1985 and early 1986, borrowers were dancing on their loan-repayment books. For the first time in more than 7 years, long-term, fixed-rate home loans again were available in the 9 percent to 10 percent range. Some 70 percent of the home loans originated in 1986 carried fixed rates as home sales soared and refinancing began to gather steam. Even borrowers with 2-year-old ARMs joined in the fun, as the rates on their loans actually declined.

What caused interest rates to tumble?

Most economists agree that Reaganomics' curbing of inflation brought down all interest rates. After several years of inflation at far less than 5 percent a year, even the most cynical observers began to believe that double-digit price increases wouldn't return quickly.

RATES AND OIL PRICES

The decline in oil prices also played a major role. In the 1970s, soaring oil prices were blamed for the surge in interest rates. Experts say the decline in oil prices reinforced the notion of economic stability. Passage by

Congress of the Gramm-Rudman Act, which aims to curb deficit spending, also gave a psychological lift to those who doubted that balancing the budget was really a goal of the Reagan administration.

Also, the Federal Reserve Board helped bring interest rates down with a monetary policy that allowed enough money to flow into the system to keep the economy moving but—the Fed hoped—not enough to create an inflationary condition in which too many dollars chase too few goods.

So, investors and bank depositors are accepting sharply lower interest rates for their money. As a result, lenders can afford to reduce their rates on new mortgages. They still can maintain a profit margin between the interest they pay out and what they charge.

Lenders also have been freed of some of the risk in making long-term, fixed-rate home loans, because a strong secondary mortgage market has been created.

Another phenomenon helping lenders is the growing popularity of 15-year, fixed-rate loans. Because the loans are for shorter terms than 30-year loans, the lender has more of its money back sooner. This reduces the impact inflation will have on the loans.

CHAPTER 4

HOW MUCH HOUSE CAN YOU AFFORD?

Home buying, especially in a boom market, can be feverish and frightening. First-timers and experienced buyers alike start out with sweaty palms.

With For Sale signs and furnished models swirling in their heads, house hunters wonder what the best buys are: A vintage condo or a two-flat close to transportation in the city? A new single-family home or a town house in a fast-growing suburb?

Before you dive headfirst into the house hunt, you should know how much home you can afford. Buying a home usually involves coming up with a substantial cash down payment and qualifying for a mortgage to cover the balance of the purchase.

You should know the amount of down payment you'll need, and where you'll get it. You'll need to know how big a mortgage you can obtain and have some idea about the other costs of home ownership. You must have these facts and figures to be able to compute how much house you can afford.

The down payment will vary depending on the way the transaction is structured and the type of financing you obtain. Conservative lenders require 20 percent of the purchase price as a down payment on a conventional loan. On a $100,000 house, you would have to have $20,000 in cash. However, if you have good credit and enough income, and if the house is worth the price, most lenders will take a 10 percent down payment, or $10,000 on that $100,000 house.

If you qualify for an FHA loan, the minimum down payment is only 5 percent. However, you also will have to pay a government mortgage insurance premium. Check the FHA loan maximum in your area. In big cities such as New York or San Francisco, it's $90,000, but it is substantially less in smaller towns. If you are a veteran of the U.S. armed services, it is possible to obtain a Veterans Administration–guaranteed loan with no money down.

CASH FOR CLOSING

Sources for Down Payment Cash

Take a minute here to calculate how much money you have available for closing costs and a down payment. Your down payment has a direct relationship to the price of home you can afford and the type of financing you should seek. The following worksheet will help you outline the available assets and funds you have to tap for your down payment.

Savings	$_____
Equity in present home (minus selling costs)	_____
Equity in other property	_____
Investments (current value)	_____
Life insurance (cash value)	_____
Cash from relatives	_____
Total available funds	$_____

From this total amount, you will have to pay closing costs. Also, it's wise to set aside money for moving expenses, new furniture, and repairs or rehab costs that often arise during the first year in a new home. You also may want to keep some cash in case of emergencies.

It is an excellent idea for a home buyer to hire an independent engineer or home inspector to check the property for termites and potential structural and mechanical defects. This usually costs $250. Attach a rider assuring the inspector's approval to the sales contract on the house. The rider is a stipulation that the offer is based on the home passing inspection.

Private Mortgage Insurance

If your down payment is less than 20 percent, the lender will require you to pay a private mortgage insurance premium.

By paying PMI, the borrower is protecting the *lender* for the difference between the down payment and 20 percent of the home's price, in case of default. Don't confuse PMI with life insurance; PMI merely protects the lender.

With a 10 percent down payment, you would have to pay 0.5 percent of the mortgage amount at closing to cover the first year's premium. On the $90,000 mortgage, that's $450.

The second year's PMI with a 10 percent down payment will be 0.34 percent of the loan balance, but you will pay it during the first year because the premium is due at the beginning of the second year. On the $90,000 loan, it would be about $300—paid in 12 monthly installments of about $25, said John Ochotnicky, vice president of Mortgage Guaranty Insurance Corp., Milwaukee, Wisconsin.

If you place a 5 percent down payment, the initial insurance premium is 1.25 percent of the loan amount, or $1,125 at closing on the $90,000 mortgage. The second year's PMI would be 0.44 of the loan balance, payable in 12 monthly installments. That's about $33 a month.

On a 15 percent down payment, the initial insurance premium is 0.35 percent of the loan amount, or $315 at closing. In the second year PMI would be based on 0.34 percent of the loan balance, or about $25 a month. In Texas and Pennsylvania, slightly higher renewal premium percentages are used. Check with local lenders.

The PMI premium is held in escrow by the lender and paid to the mortgage insurance company at the beginning of each year.

PMI payments usually continue until you have paid off enough of the mortgage to reach 20 percent equity of the purchase price. Many lenders will not consider a home's appreciation—and thus your increased equity—unless you refinance.

On a $100,000 home with a 30-year fixed-rate mortgage, it would take about 9 years to reach 20 percent equity after making a 15 percent down payment. With 10 percent down, it would take 12 or 13 years. With a 5 percent down payment, it would take 15 years—half the mortgage's length. That's because the lion's share of early-year mortgage payments go to interest, not principal.

PMI premiums are reviewed at the end of 10 years and adjustments are made for principal paid down, said Ochotnicky. On the $90,000 loan with 10 percent down, the monthly PMI premium could drop to $9 from $25 in the 11th year and stay there until 20 percent equity is reached in year 12 or 13.

Don't Overlook Closing Costs

Many first-time buyers—and those homeowners who bought homes before points became so prevalent—tend to overlook closing costs. But they are a major expense and can drastically cut into your down payment nest egg.

The largest closing cost usually is points, or special loan fees lenders charge to increase their profits. One point equals 1 percent of the mortgage amount. So, if a lender charges 3 points on a $90,000 mortgage, you will have to pay $2,700 at closing.

Some lenders will lower the interest rate on a loan if you will pay more points at closing. It is unusual today to find a lender willing to charge no points without raising the annual rate. Also, if you want to lock in the interest rate being offered at the time you apply, you usually will have to pay 0.5 to 1 point.

Points will make the annual percentage rate (APR) of your loan appear higher than originally quoted on the loan documents. You'll learn more about APR in Chapter 7.

In addition to the down payment and points, you may have to pay other major closing costs on a conventional loan. However, some of the charges listed may not apply to your transaction:

Loan Application Fee. Typically $250 to $275, the loan application fee usually covers the cost of the appraisal and credit report.

Loan Origination Fee. Expect to pay 1 percent of the loan amount, or $900 on a $90,000 loan, for a loan origination fee if you want to lock in the interest rate on your mortgage. If you float the rate and take the market level at closing, you won't pay this fee. The fee is like a point in every way but one: It's not tax-deductible.

Private Mortgage Insurance. If you put less than 20 percent down, you will have to prepay the first private mortgage insurance premium at closing. If you place 5 percent down, the first year's fee would be 1.25 percent of the loan amount. With 10 percent down, the fee would be 0.5 percent of the mortgage amount. If you put down 15 percent, the fee would be 0.35 percent.

Initial Mortgage Payment. The lender will require a buyer to pay the first month's mortgage payment at closing. On a $90,000 loan for 30 years at 10 percent, that would be $790.

Title Search and Insurance. The cost for a title search and insurance typically runs about $400. The title policy, usually issued by a title insurance company, assures payment to any claimant in case of discrepancies in the title to the property. If you are buying a home, the fee usually is paid by the seller or split between buyer and seller.

Property Survey. A current survey, which costs $75 to $150, checks property lines to make sure that there are no encroachments on your land that might hamper a future sale. Usually it is paid for by the seller.

Deed Recording. This fee of $25 to $35 covers legally recording a deed with the proper governmental authorities.

Recording Taxes. Some local governments charge a stamp tax based on the amount of the sales transaction. A typical amount is $250.

Document Preparation. All that paper shuffling, including notary services, costs money. Figure about $50.

Prepaid Homeowner's Insurance. Generally, the lender requires the buyer to pay the first year's homeowners' insurance premium at or before closing. The cost is $250 to $400.

Prorated Property Taxes. If you buy a house and close

on June 30, for example, you will be responsible for half of the year's taxes and insurance. If the seller already paid these costs for the whole year, he or she will get a rebate from you at closing. If this year's property taxes are payable next year, you will receive a prorated credit from the seller at closing.

Lawyer Fees. The attorney's fees will be about $250 to $500. Expect to pay higher legal fees on a condominium closing because of the added paper work.

Closing Cost Summary

Once you have a home picked out, use this handy checklist to tally up actual closing costs.

Loan application fee	$ _200_
Loan origination fee	_450_
Private mortgage insurance	_300_
Initial mortgage payment	_514_
Title search and insurance	_400_
Property survey	_100_
Deed recording	_25_
Prepaid homeowners' insurance	_250_
Prorated property taxes	_250_
Lawyer fee	_200_
Total	$ _____

If you pay normal points and closing costs and don't lock in your mortgage rate, total closing costs on a $90,000 loan could easily be more than $4,000. When you add that to the $10,000 down payment, that's an out-of-pocket expense of $14,000 to step across the threshold of a $100,000 home.

Of course, substantial tax benefits are associated with home ownership. Details of the savings will be discussed at the end of this chapter.

FINANCING

Qualifying for a Mortgage

When figuring how much housing debt you can comfortably carry, the lender depends largely on two factors: the interest rate on the loan and your income.

The mortgage amount, term, and interest rate determine your monthly loan payment. The higher the interest rate, the higher the monthly payment. Your net monthly income, less any substantial debts such as a car payment, determines how much you can spend for a mortgage.

Lenders have general rules of thumb. They say your mortgage principal and interest payments should not exceed 25 percent of your gross monthly income. When real estate taxes and homeowners' insurance are added, your monthly payments for principal, interest, taxes, and insurance (PITI) should not exceed 28 percent of your gross income. Total housing costs plus other long-term debts, such as car payments, student loans, and credit-card obligations, should not exceed 33 percent of the buyers' total gross monthly income.

If you can qualify within these guidelines, you should be able to afford a home. However, some families prefer to take on payments well below the maximum allowed.

These qualification standards usually serve both the borrower and the lender, helping both avoid a situation that could lead to a default.

What Can You Afford?

Before you buy a house and take on the burden of home-loan payments, you should calculate the maximum monthly mortgage payment you can afford and the total amount of down payment you have, less closing costs. These figures will help you figure the size of your mortgage and how much house you can afford.

Use the following mortgage worksheet to calculate how much house you can afford. The bottom line, maximum purchase price, will tell you how expensive a house you can qualify for.

When computing your gross monthly income, don't forget other sources of cash. Do you earn cash from a steady part-time job? Do you earn interest and dividends on investments, or make money on rent or leases?

Figure the mortgage payment you can afford:

If you know your family's gross monthly
   pay, write it on Line (1). If you don't
   know it, multiply gross weekly pay
   (before deductions) by 4.33. The result is
   gross monthly income.
Gross monthly income = weekly pay
   _____ × 4.33 = $_2199_ (1)

Lenders say your monthly mortgage
   payment for principal and interest
   cannot be more than 25 percent of your
   gross monthly income. Multiply the
   amount on Line (1) by 0.25. The result
   is the payment you can afford.
Gross monthly payment you can afford =
   Line (1) _2199_ × 0.25 = $_549.75_ (2)
For simplicity, we are assuming that your monthly payment for taxes, homeowners' insurance and PMI will be about 3 percent of your gross monthly income.

Net monthly payment you can afford:

Now that you know how much you can afford to pay, take a look at the payment tables on pages 29 and 30 to see how large a 15-year or 30-year fixed-rate mortgage you can handle. To use the tables, you need to know the current range of interest rates (look in your local newspaper or call a lender or two).

Payments for Principal and Interest on a 30-Year Mortgage

Interest rate	$50,000	$60,000	$70,000	$80,000	$90,000	$100,000	$120,000	$150,000
				Principal Amount				
8.5%	$384	$461	$538	$615	$693	$771	$923	$1,153
9.0	402	483	563	644	724	805	966	1,207
9.5	420	505	589	673	757	841	1,009	1,261
10.0	439	527	614	702	790	878	1,053	1,316
10.5	457	549	640	732	823	915	1,098	1,372
11.0	476	571	667	762	857	952	1,143	1,428
11.5	495	594	693	792	891	990	1,188	1,485
12.0	514	617	720	823	926	1,029	1,234	1,543
12.5	534	640	747	854	961	1,067	1,281	1,601

Payments for Principal and Interest on a 15-Year Mortgage

Interest rate	$50,000	$60,000	$70,000	$80,000	$90,000	$100,000	$120,000	$150,000
				Principal Amount				
8.5%	$492	$592	$689	$787	$886	$984	$1,171	$1,476
9.0	507	609	710	811	913	1,014	1,217	1,521
9.5	522	627	731	835	940	1,044	1,253	1,566
10.0	537	645	752	860	967	1,075	1,290	1,612
10.5	553	663	774	884	995	1,105	1,326	1,658
11.0	568	682	796	909	1,023	1,137	1,364	1,705
11.5	584	701	818	935	1,051	1,168	1,402	1,752
12.0	600	720	840	960	1,080	1,200	1,440	1,800
12.5	616	740	863	986	1,109	1,233	1,479	1,849

Choose the table for a 30-year loan (page 29) or a 15-year loan (page 30). Look across the line with the prevailing interest rate until you find a monthly payment near what you can pay. If the table does not go high enough for your income, a more complete table can be found in the Appendix. Then, look up to the top of the chart to find the mortgage amount.

Enter this amount—the maximum
   mortgage amount—on Line (3). $ _80000_ (3)

Gross cash available:

  Now that you know the mortgage amount you can afford, figure out how much you will have to pay in closing costs. That will let you know how much is left for a down payment.

On Line (4), enter the total amount of
   cash you have set aside for the down
   payment, inspection fee, moving
   expenses, repairs, emergencies, and
   closing costs: $___.00 (4)

Subtract $250 for the home inspection fee.
   Enter the answer on Line 5:
Line (4) _____ – $250 = $ _–250_ (5)

Subtract from Line (5) the money you will
   keep for moving expenses, initial home
   repairs, and emergencies. Enter the
   answer on Line (6):
Available funds = Line (5) _____ –
_____ = $_____ (6)

Multiply the mortgage amount from Line (3) by 0.045, the average total closing costs. Enter your estimated total closing costs on Line (7):

Closing costs = Line (3) _____ × 0.045 = $_3600_ (7)

Net cash available for down payment:

To find net cash available for down payment, subtract closing costs on Line (7) from the available funds on Line (6). Enter amount available for down payment on Line (8):

Amount available for down payment = Line (6) _____ – Line (7) _____ = $_____ (8)

Maximum home cost—the bottom line:

To figure the maximum purchase price of a home you can afford, add the maximum mortgage amount from Line (3) and the maximum down payment from Line (8). Enter the answer—the maximum purchase price—on Line (9):

Maximum purchase price = Line (3) _____ + Line (8) _____ = $_____ (9)

CHAPTER 5

ALL THE COSTS OF HOME OWNERSHIP

A mortgage payment is only part of the cost of home ownership. So far you've figured out roughly how much you can afford to pay for a house.

Once you find a specific home you are interested in, the worksheets in this chapter will help you estimate all housing costs, including utilities and maintenance. Perhaps you should skim this chapter now and return to it once you have a specific house in mind.

If you have a budget like this one ready, you'll be fairly well-prepared for a qualifying interview at the bank, savings and loan association, or mortgage broker.

MONTHLY HOUSING COSTS

Use the following six-step guide included in this chapter and the handy loan amortization tables in the Appendix to estimate total monthly housing payments, including principal and interest payments, real estate taxes, homeowners' insurance, monthly utility bills, and maintenance costs.

33

Monthly Mortgage Cost
Per Thousand Dollars

This table shows the monthly cost of borrowing per $1,000 at various interest rates.

Interest Rate	15-Year Loan	30-Year Loan
8.0%	$ 9.56	$ 7.34
8.5	9.85	7.69
9.0	10.15	8.05
9.5	10.45	8.41
10.0	10.75	8.78
10.5	11.06	9.15
11.0	11.37	9.53
11.5	11.69	9.91
12.0	12.01	10.29
12.5	12.33	10.68
13.0	12.66	11.07
13.5	12.99	11.46
14.0	13.32	11.85
14.5	13.66	12.25
15.0	14.00	12.65

First fill in this basic information:

Home purchase price $ _80000_

Mortgage amount (principal minus down payment) $ _'00_

Mortgage interest rate   _8½_ %

Term of loan   _15_ yrs.

STEP 1

To determine loan amount in thousands, divide the mortgage amount by 1,000 and enter the result on Line (1).

Loan amount _80 000_ ÷ 1,000 = _80_ (1)

In the table on page 340, find the cost per
$1,000 for your mortgage's interest rate
and term. (For example, if the rate is 10
percent and the term is 30 years, the cost
per $1,000 is $8.78.)
Enter the cost per $1,000 on Line (2)   ___9.85___ (2)

To find the monthly principal and interest
payment, multiply mortgage amount (in
thousands) from Line (1) by the cost per
$1,000 from Line (2). Enter the answer
on Line (3):
Monthly payment = Line (1) ___80___ ×
Line (2) ___9.85___ =   ___788___ (3)

STEP 2

To figure monthly cost for the property
tax, enter annual property taxes and
divide by 12. Enter your answer on Line
(4):
Annual taxes _____ ÷ 12 =   _____ (4)

STEP 3

To figure monthly homeowners' insurance
costs, enter the yearly cost of
homeowners' insurance and divide by
12. Enter your answer on Line (5):
Annual insurance _____ ÷ 12 =   _____ (5)

STEP 4

Estimates for the home's monthly heating,
electricity, water, and garbage pickup
bills should be available from the seller.
Telephone costs should be based on your
current expenses. Enter this information
on the following lines:

Natural gas or oil   _____ (6)
Electricity   _____ (7)
Water   _____ (8)
Telephone   _____ (9)
Garbage collection   _____ (10)
Total utilities = total of lines (6), (7), (8),
    (9), (10) =   _____ (11)

STEP 5

A rule of thumb is that annual
    maintenance costs equal about 1 percent
    of the home's price. To estimate yearly
    maintenance and repairs, multiply the
    home's sale price by .01. The monthly
    expense is that amount divided by 12.
    Enter the monthly amount on Line (12).
Price _____ × .01 ÷ 12 =   _____ (12)

STEP 6

Now let's put those monthly housing costs
    together. Add the following figures:
Mortgage payment from Line (3)   _____
Property taxes from Line (4)   _____
Insurance costs from Line (5)   _____
Utility costs from Line (11)   _____
Maintenance costs from Line (12)   _____
Add these amounts to get the bottom line,
    total monthly home ownership costs. $_____ (13)

HOME BUDGET WORKSHEET

Now that you know what it will cost to put a roof
over your head, it's time to look at some of your
family's other spending habits and preferences. This
will give you a bottom-line assessment of whether
you'll be eating franks and beans every night for the
privilege of owning a home.

Average monthly nonhousing expenses:

Food   _____

Clothing   _____

Transportation, including car costs   _____

Life insurance   _____

Health insurance   _____

Medical and dental care   _____

Education   _____

Installment payments   _____

Savings, emergency funds   _____

Entertainment and recreation   _____

Vacations   _____

Charity   _____

Pocket money   _____

Other: _____

    Total nonhousing expenses   \$_____ (14)

Now add your total monthly nonhousing
    expenses to your total monthly housing
    expenses from Line (13).

Line (13) _____ + Line (14)

_____ =   \$_____ (15)

Compare the total on Line (15) to your total monthly
take-home pay. If you are signing up to shell out more
than you bring in, relax for a minute. The U.S.
Congress knows it's expensive to be a homeowner. So
realizing that homeowners also are voters, the good
people in Washington, D.C., created income tax deductions that make this whole situation a lot easier to take.

COMPUTING INCOME TAX SAVINGS

The true out-of-pocket cost of owning a home can't
really be computed until you deduct tax savings from
your monthly payment.

First of all, points paid separately at closing are deductible from federally taxable income in the year paid. This is a one-time fee and a one-time deduction. The other two major tax advantages of home ownership—the deductibility of mortgage interest and property taxes—provide annual assistance.

The amount of tax savings created by the deductions is based on the individual homeowner's tax bracket. Of course, your actual monthly payments do not change. The savings come once a year at income tax time from the deductions you claim.

For example, let's suppose a married couple in the 38 percent tax bracket took out a $90,000 mortgage. (Based on 1986 tax rates, they would have a joint taxable annual income of between $49,420 and $64,749.)

The couple paid $2,700 in points to close their $90,000 mortgage. Assuming they file a joint tax return, they could deduct the full $2,700 from their 1986 income, providing a tax savings of $1,026 (.38 × $2,700). Similarly, they could deduct 38 percent of their mortgage interest payments and property taxes, so their annual tax savings would be substantial.

Use the following guide to estimate what the *real* monthly cost will be for your home after allowable tax deductions:

STEP 1: Figuring your monthly tax deduction

To estimate monthly tax deductions on
  mortgage interest, multiply the monthly
  principal and interest payment from
  Line (3) by .97. (That's because at least
  97 percent of your first-year payments is
  tax-deductible.) Enter answer on Line (16):
Line (3) ___788___ × .97 =   ___764___ (16)
Enter your monthly property tax payment
  on Line (17)   _____ (17)
To figure total monthly deductions, add

Lines (16) and (17). Enter your answer
on Line 18:

Line (16) _____ + Line (17)

_____ =   _____ (18)

STEP 2: Figuring your tax savings

To figure your monthly tax savings,
multiply your monthly tax deductions
from Line (18) by your marginal tax
rate. To find your tax rate, look under
the appropriate filing status in the tax
table on page 40. For example, a couple
filing jointly with annual income of
$55,000 has a tax rate of 0.38. Enter
your answer on Line (19):

Monthly tax savings = Line (18)

_____ × tax rate

_____ =   _____ (19)

STEP 3: After-tax housing cost

To figure your after-tax monthly housing
cost, subtract your tax savings on Line
(19) from your total monthly home
ownership costs on Line (13). Enter the
answer on Line (20):

Line (13) _____ − Line (19)

_____ =   _____ (20)

STEP 4: Total after-tax monthly cash outlay

To figure your after-tax monthly cash
outlay, add your after-tax monthly
housing costs on Line (20) to your total
nonhousing expenses on Line (14).
Enter your answer on Line (21):

After-tax monthly outlay = Line (20)

_____ + Line (14)

_____ =   _____ (21)

Marginal Tax Rates

Married Couples Filing Joint Returns		Single Persons	
Taxable Income	Tax Rate	Taxable Income	Tax Rate
$17,270–$21,799	.18	$13,920–$16,189	.20
21,800–26,549	.22	16,190–19,639	.23
26,550–32,269	.25	19,640–25,359	.26
32,270–37,979	.28	25,360–31,079	.30
37,980–49,419	.33	31,080–36,799	.34
49,420–64,749	.38	36,800–44,779	.38
64,750–92,369	.42	44,780–59,669	.42
92,370–118,049	.45	59,670–88,269	.48
118,050–175,249	.49	88,270+	.50
175,250+	.50		

Source: Internal Revenue Service.

Note: Tax rates are for 1986. Check with IRS for exact figures for future years.

Now compare the after-tax monthly cash outlay you just figured to your monthly take-home pay. That looks a lot better, doesn't it? Clearly, the tax advantages make home ownership a lot easier to afford. If you still would be spending more than you're taking in, look carefully at your nonhousing expenses. Perhaps you can cut down on some of them. Home ownership will make it worthwhile.

There is one final point about the after-tax impact of home ownership. As mentioned before, the deductions are taken only once a year at tax time. (The illustration here uses monthly tax saving to make the impact easier to see.) You have to pay out the amount on Line (13) each month.

You probably would be wise to reduce the amount withheld from your paycheck for federal income tax so you can meet your bills. This makes sense because your interest and property-tax deductions will reduce your annual federal income tax.

CHAPTER 6

HOW TO START SHOPPING FOR A MORTGAGE

The late 1980s look like a good time to buy a home. Although home prices are increasing, interest rates are relatively stable in most cities around the country.

There's no telling if or when long-term fixed rates will dip below 10 percent again, but if you've been watching the housing market during the past few years, you know that today's rates are far better than what was available early in this decade.

If you completed the worksheet in Chapter 4, you know how much house you can afford. Once you decide to buy a home, selecting the right type of mortgage for your pocketbook and qualifying for it constitute the next step.

"In the good old days, the head of the neighborhood savings and loan would look you over with a squint. If you looked like an all-right guy, he'd make the loan," said Chicago real estate lawyer Marshall J. Moltz. "Today, the borrower is a voice on a telephone, and there are many more financial requirements and approval documents. Everything is fed into a computer, and applying for a mortgage is much more impersonal."

As Moltz points out, seeking a loan has changed dramatically. In fact, shopping for a home loan today is like scanning the menu at a fancy French restaurant. Lenders not only have a wide assortment of products to peddle, but some of their offerings may seem foreign to you. So it pays to know your way around the mortgage marketplace before you start.

SHOP AROUND

The amount you pay each month for your home mortgage depends, in part, on the type of mortgage you select and the prevailing interest rate. But it also can be affected by the lending institution you choose.

One lender may charge a slightly lower rate than another for an identical mortgage. Another might charge a slightly higher rate, but fewer points. Application fees and other closing costs for similar loans also can vary from lender to lender.

So, if you are short on cash for a down payment, choose the lender who charges a slightly higher rate, but fewer points. Because you are spending such a large amount of money, it is essential that you shop around—comparing rates, terms, and closing costs— before choosing a mortgage and a lender.

Lenders are eager to make mortgages, because loans generate new fee and servicing income. And, lenders say, borrowers who finance homes at today's lower rates usually are better credit risks and less likely to default than those facing the 15 percent rates of the early '80s.

THE LOAN RUSH

When loan rates are low—especially after extended periods of substantially higher rates—mortgage makers tend to be very busy. In early 1986, when mortgage rates tumbled to nearly 9 percent from more than 12 percent a year earlier, millions of Americans rushed to buy houses or refinance high-interest home loans.

But the magic of single-digit interest rates created a stampede that buried appraisal, survey, and credit companies in an avalanche of work. Three months after applying for a loan, some borrowers still hadn't been able to close their deals.

If loan applications are pouring in, you might be put on a waiting list just for an appointment. Getting an appraisal of the home—necessary for the lender—can take five to ten weeks, instead of the two weeks usual in a normal housing market.

A credit report, usually issued in days, can take five weeks during a mortgage boom, and a property survey that usually takes one week can take six times as long. Heavy application volume in 1986 caused some lenders to extend interest-rate commitments to 75 days on a conventional loan and 90 days on government-insured mortgages. In a normal year, the total process can be completed in 30 to 45 days.

In 1986, borrowers complained that some mortgage brokers let rate commitments expire, then increased rates to reflect recently increased interest charges. But mortgage bankers and brokers said they had no choice. Investors wanted the highest yields possible and refused to honor expired commitments for single-digit mortgages when higher rates were available.

During 1986, alleged rate gouging and fee churning in the mortgage banking industry sparked investigations by state regulators in Illinois, Maryland, and Massachusetts. At the same time, many banks and S&Ls were honoring expired commitments—and making some lifelong customers.

"Often there's much more red tape and extra cost dealing with out-of-state lenders—mortgage bankers and brokers who sell their loans to investors," said Moltz.

WHERE TO START
THE HOME-LOAN HUNT

Mortgage experts give the following home-loan shopping list for families starting the mortgage hunt:

Look in your own backyard. Based on the mortgage brokers' track record in 1986, some analysts recommend paying a slightly higher rate and going to a bank or S&L, which likely will be more customer oriented.

Begin at your neighborhood S&L or bank. It could prove to be the best place to get a loan, especially if you are an established customer. If you are not a customer, become one. Most lenders want to keep their loyal customers.

However, don't assume your lender has the best deals. Check around. Some lenders charge higher rates because they aren't all that interested in home mortgages.

Don't be overanxious. Don't get locked into accepting the first loan you're offered without making certain it's the best available at the time. With the frequent fluctuation of rates these days, no lender has the best deal even half the time.

Shop around. Although it may be fun to shop for bargain prices on consumer products, it can be even more rewarding if you take the time to find a mortgage deal. Get quotations from at least three lending institutions, and preferably many more. A few extra phone calls could save you hundreds of dollars.

For example, if you inquire at a bank or S&L around April 15—right after the federal income tax deadline— you might find the institution loaded with cash from Individual Retirement Account deposits. In farm communities, a lender may be flush soon after harvest. Some S&Ls also have a glut of money from loan repayments sparked by refinancing.

If you find an eager lender, you may be able to

negotiate a lower mortgage rate, and there also may be lower point charges. Even a reduction of 0.25 percentage points in the interest rate can represent a savings of thousands of dollars over the life of a fixed-rate loan.

Compare more than just interest rates. Ask what other charges you will have to pay. These could include points, loan origination fee, application fee, appraisal fee, and many more charges. And don't forget to ask friends and business associates about the lender's reputation. In 1986, some lenders earned dubious achievement awards for bumbling mortgage processing and allowing delays that cost borrowers thousands of dollars in fees and higher monthly payments.

Consider shorter mortgages. Don't be afraid of shorter-term loans. At the lower rates available in 1986, thousands of borrowers took on shorter-term loans.

Picking a 15-year loan over a 30-year loan will mean higher monthly payments, but the savings on interest could amount to tens of thousands of dollars, and the gain in equity will be substantial. On a $50,000 loan at 10 percent for 15 years, you would owe $40,650 after 5 years. Had you chosen a 30-year loan at 10 percent, you would owe $48,300 after 5 years.

The difference is even more dramatic after 15 years. You would be holding a mortgage-burning party for that 15-year loan, but you'd still owe $40,850 on the 30-year mortgage. (To find out the equity buildup with each loan, see the mortgage progress table in the Appendix.)

Beware of rate fluctuations. It is important to ask exactly when the rate you are applying for will be established. With rates fluctuating daily, a homeowner should determine whether the contract rate will be the one available on the day of the application or the one available on the day of the actual closing.

Some banks may charge up to a full point extra if a homeowner wants to lock in a rate. When rates are stable or moving lower, it is a good idea to apply for a loan and let the rate float until closing. There's no sense in paying to lock in a rate when interest charges may go lower.

Ask questions. It pays to inquire about different loan programs because lenders now are offering so many new types of mortgage instruments. The programs vary from one institution to another. But don't accept a loan you don't want. If a bank or S&L says it will give you only an adjustable-rate mortgage, and you don't want that, go elsewhere.

Don't forget to ask about government-backed loan programs. Ask your realty agent if the house you plan to buy is eligible for an FHA-insured loan. Eligibility depends on a maximum price level by geographic region. For example, in the Chicago area the maximum FHA-loan amount is $87,250. In New York and San Francisco it's $90,000. If you or your spouse served in the military, you may be eligible for a no-money-down Veterans Administration–guaranteed loan.

Mortage lenders have more types of loans to offer than ever before, but many of them may not be for you. Pros and cons of some of the most popular home financing options available at S&Ls, banks, and mortgage companies will be discussed starting in Chapter 8.

Don't wait forever. In every interest-rate cycle, some borrowers want to wait until rates hit bottom. Don't worry about getting the absolutely lowest rate. Experts say borrowers should cut their financing deal when rates are in the trough of the cycle—not when they start to head up.

When even Wall Street's wizards can't figure how low—or high—rates will go, the best advice is to take a deal that makes financial sense. Your rate may not be absolutely the lowest, but you will have a home you can afford.

MORTGAGE QUIZ
REQUIRES HOMEWORK

The lender you select will have two basic questions: First, can you come up with the down payment for the mortgage? Second, can you afford the monthly payment, including principal, interest, taxes, and homeowners' insurance?

The boom housing market and refinancing craze buried lenders under a mountain of mortgage applications in 1986. When rates are affordable, borrowers must work harder to help lenders get their loan approved.

Of course, lenders will ask how much money you need to borrow and for how long. But there also will be questions about your monthly income, bank balance and debts, age, marital status, and number of dependents.

Getting Personal

Questions involving economics sometimes may seem personal to a sensitive applicant. For example, the home-loan application required by the Federal Home Loan Mortgage Corporation (Freddie Mac) and the Federal National Mortgage Association (Fannie Mae) ask the following penetrating questions:

1. Have you been declared bankrupt in the last seven years?
2. Are there any outstanding judgments against you?
3. Was your property foreclosed upon, or did you give title or deed in lieu of foreclosure?
4. Are you a co-maker or endorser on a note?
5. Are you obligated to pay alimony, child support, or separate maintenance?
6. Is any part of the down payment borrowed?

Another sensitive area is marital status. Lenders say that the traditional family unit—working husband, homemaker wife, and one or more children—is no longer traditional. In fact, this structure now comprises the minority of home buyers.

Loan underwriters and realty agents see all types of shared-housing situations and make no distinction among them. At times, people may become uncomfortable about disclosing their relationship with a co-buyer.

Again, this is an economic issue. If you are a co-buyer in a nontraditional relationship, it might be wise to consult with an attorney to determine the legal ramifications of the partnership and how title of the property should be held.

Under the law, certain personal questions are forbidden, including whether the applicant is a U.S. citizen, has a police record, or belongs to any clubs, social organizations, or trade or service organizations.

Questions the Borrower Should Ask

Don't let the lender ask all the questions. The dollars you owe can change for each mortgage option a lender offers. Of course, you should ask basic questions about application and loan origination fees, interest rate, loan term, points, down payment, mortgage amount, and private mortgage insurance.

But there are other questions you should ask. Make copies of the following list of questions, and use it as a guide when comparing various mortgages and lenders:

1. Will I be required to pay into a special escrow account each month to cover property taxes and homeowners' insurance?
2. Can the original term of the loan be extended?
3. Is there a grace period beyond a payment's due

date, and is there a late payment charge on
monthly payments?

4. Is there a prepayment penalty if I wish to pay off
   the entire loan in advance of maturity? What are
   the terms of the penalty?

5. If I prepay principal, how do I know how much
   of each future payment is principal and how
   much is interest? Do I receive an annual
   accounting of principal owed?

6. Can the loan be assumed by another qualified
   borrower? Does the lender have the right, upon
   assumption, to raise the rate of interest or charge
   an assumption fee?

7. Do the terms of the loan permit me to borrow
   additional money on the mortgage after I have
   paid off part of the original loan?

8. If I must pay private mortgage insurance, when
   can I stop paying it? Will the lender alert me, or
   do I have to watch for it myself?

SPEEDING YOUR MORTGAGE APPROVAL

Experts say the best way to survive the tedium of
mortgage qualification is to be prepared for everything
when you visit the lender.

"Homeowners can help speed loan approval by
carefully collecting the pertinent financial data and
making sure the loan officer gets it quickly," said
mortgage analyst Gary S. Meyers, president of Chi-
cago-based Gary S. Meyers & Associates.

What to Bring

Here are some tips and a list of documents and
financial information you'll need when you apply for a
mortgage.

Your Checkbook. When you first apply, most institutions will charge $250 to $275 to process a loan application. The money goes for a credit report and appraisal. They often won't start the wheels moving until it's paid.

Credit Report. Before you apply for a loan, it's well worth the fee to hire a reputable credit reporting agency to conduct your credit check. This will alert you to any surprises or mistakes listed in your credit background.

And, while you are hunting for a lender, the credit work will be under way. When you apply for the loan, you can notify the lender that the report is completed. If you don't know of such an agency in your area, ask potential lenders which agency they use. Then contact the agency directly.

Employment Verification. You will be asked to sign a verification form that will be sent to your employer. The form verifies that you are employed in good standing. Know the name of a person at your company who verifies employment and alert him or her that an inquiry is coming. If you've been with your current company for less than two years, you should have the same information and personnel contact with your former employer.

Proof of Income. You will need your federal income tax returns for the past two years, especially if you are self-employed. When quoting current or expected income, be sure to include any commissions, bonuses, or regular overtime pay. Child support and alimony also should be shown, whether you give it or get it.

Bank Accounts. Ask your savings institution for a statement showing that you have enough cash for the down payment and closing costs in your account. You also will have to provide account or certificate numbers for your checking and savings accounts, as well as the addresses of the financial institutions.

It's also a good idea to list any stock or bond holdings, because they increase your financial standing in the lender's eyes. Find out where the institutions give out credit information. It may be the main office, not the branch office you usually deal with.

Credit Cards. Give account numbers of all your major cards. Make sure all accounts are current, and clean up any delinquencies before you apply for the loan.

Outstanding Loans. You must provide the account number and addresses of all lenders. This includes real estate and personal loans.

Previous Loans. If you've paid off other loans, including student loans, list them and the lender. Credit companies often lack the information and don't report loans that are paid off. Make sure you get credit for having paid off loans.

Copies of All Documents. When supplying a lender with information, do not send original documents; copies are acceptable. To avoid delays, any papers mailed should be sent with a return-receipt request and be addressed to a specific person at the lending institution.

Questionable Debts. If you have any questionable debts, or there are any special circumstances regarding your credit background, tell the loan officer. Anything out of the ordinary that shows up on your credit report must be explained. Make it as easy as possible for a busy loan officer to approve your mortgage.

Know the Limits

To help protect themselves—and the borrower—financial institutions across the nation have tightened their credit requirements and limited the total debt borrowers are allowed to carry and still receive loan approval.

The limits are now 28 percent of *gross* income for mortgage payments, including principal, interest, taxes, and homeowners' insurance, and 33 percent of total debt, including credit cards and auto loans. This means that if your gross income is $2,000 per month, the highest monthly mortgage payment you may qualify for is $560 per month. Your total monthly debt payment may not exceed $660 per month.

CHAPTER 7

READING THE FINE PRINT

Before you put your signature on the dotted line of a sales contract for a home and all those legal documents needed to take out a mortgage, ask a real estate lawyer or other expert to help you interpret the fine print.

Like most legally binding documents, sales contracts and mortgage papers contain complex terms that a bricklayer, junior executive, or astronaut might not understand.

SALES CONTRACT CLAUSES

The standard real estate contract used in most parts of the nation contains more clauses than most buyers and sellers realize. Most of the provisions are negotiable—from the selling price to who pays for the termite inspection.

Hassles abound in real estate transactions, because many buyers and sellers don't read the contract's fine print. For example, a young couple signed a contract to purchase a vintage home in an area that had been reassessed and hit with a hefty real estate tax increase. However, when the buyers read the sales contract, it called for the seller to prorate the taxes based on 110 percent of the last bill, and place that amount in an escrow account.

If it were not for a sharp-eyed real estate lawyer, the first-home buyers would have been stuck with paying the part of the seller's taxes that probably will exceed 110 percent of the last tax bill. The attorney probably saved the young home buyers several hundred dollars—more than what most lawyers would charge.

"The tax proration clause in the broker's standard sales contract wasn't helpful," said Chicago real estate lawyer Marshall J. Moltz. "What if the taxes go up 50 percent? It could have cost the unsuspecting buyers hundreds of dollars."

To protect inexperienced clients, Moltz said lawyers should include a tax reproration clause in the sales contract. Then, the seller's share of the taxes can be reprorated when the bill arrives. If there isn't enough money in the escrow account, the seller would be required to pay the difference.

Subject to Attorney Approval

All too few home buyers bother to hire a real estate lawyer before they sign a contract to purchase a house. Unfortunately, most real estate sales contracts are signed, sealed, and delivered before a lawyer sees them. But it doesn't have to be that way.

Ideally, a savvy buyer would have a lawyer draft a purchase contract before papers are signed. However, if the buyer writes "subject to attorney approval" on the contract when he or she signs it, the protection will be there.

Later, the buyer's lawyer can refine the sales contract and add provisions that he or she would have included if given the chance to draft it originally.

After all, most of the fine print in a typical real estate sales contract is designed to protect the seller, not the buyer. Consequently you need a lawyer to study all that fine print and to add a few provisions that are on your side.

Experts say a buyer needs a lawyer before the closing, too. "What happens if the roof leaks or serious structural problems develop in the house? It's a real estate lawyer's job to put warranties in the contract so there is a legal basis for voiding the deal if defects occur after closing," said Moltz.

What to Cover

Your attorney should review, approve, and add necessary addenda to the contract to cover the following key points:

Tax Prorations. To compute accurate tax prorations, the buyer and seller must use the most recent tax assessment rate plus 10 percent. However, when the final installment of the tax bill is issued, the buyer and seller will reprorate the taxes and make any necessary cash adjustment.

Mortgage Contingency Provisions. If a buyer is unable to obtain a commitment for a mortgage, he or she is required to notify the seller in writing as soon as possible.

But if the buyer fails to notify the seller in writing within a certain time period, the seller should not infer that the buyer has a mortgage or has agreed to purchase the property without financing. This clause protects a buyer from losing his or her earnest money.

Plat of Survey. A survey is like an X-ray. The seller is responsible for furnishing a survey no more than six months old, showing that there are no undisclosed encroachments or easements involving the adjoining property.

The standard title insurance policy does not protect against encroachments, boundary line disputes, or anything else that could be disclosed by a survey and a property inspection.

Restrictions of Record. The buyer purchases the property only subject to restrictions of record. Although deed restrictions, such as zoning, covenants, easements, or special assessments are highly technical, buyers should be aware of them and review them in the contract.

Right to Inspect. After the contract and addendum from an attorney are signed, the purchaser has the right to inspect the property and all improvements on it. The seller may not refuse the buyer access to the property.

Evidence of Good Title. The seller must produce evidence of good title in the form of a title commitment policy. Lenders require a title commitment policy.

Building Maintenance. The seller must agree to keep the property, including the building and all other improvements, in good repair between the date of the contract and closing.

Warranty Against Defects. When a home is purchased, there is an implied warranty of habitability. On the date of closing, the seller must warrant that all mechanical systems (such as water, sewer, plumbing, heating, and electrical), as well as appliances included in the sale, are in working order. The premises also must be free of structural defects and termites or other insect infestation.

"When it comes to plumbing, I advise my clients to flush before they buy," said Moltz, who once represented a purchaser who bought a house with plumbing fixtures that were installed but not connected to the sewer system. "It's a good idea to hire a professional engineer or home inspector to check the house before you buy."

MORTGAGE FINE PRINT

Not all the fine print is in the sales contract. There are plenty of pitfalls in mortgage documents, too. For example, here is a sample *acceleration clause* taken from a mortgage contract:

> In the event any installment of this note is not paid when due, time being of the essence, and such installment remains unpaid for thirty (30) days, the Holder of this Note may, at its option, without notice or demand, declare the entire principal sum then unpaid, together with accrued interest and late charge thereon, immediately due and payable. The lender may without further notice or demand invoke the power of sale and any other remedies permitted by applicable law.

This legal jargon means if you are more than 30 days late with your mortgage payment, the lender can require you to pay immediately the entire unpaid balance of the loan. If you don't have the money, the lender could start foreclosure proceedings that eventually could lead to a sheriff's sale of your home.

Note the use of the words "without notice." If this contract provision is legal in your state, this means you have waived your right to notice of a missed mortgage payment or delinquency or default.

So, if you go on vacation to the Bahamas and forget to mail your mortgage payment—or your check is lost in the mail—the lender can initiate action against you before you are told. The lender even may start to foreclose.

Legal Tip: Know whether your mortgage contract waives your right to notice. If it does, obtain a clear understanding in advance of what you're giving up. And consider having your attorney check state law to determine whether the waiver is legal. Also, have the attorney talk to the lender about eliminating such language.

Beware of Due-on-Sale Clauses

For years, due-on-sale clauses have been included in many mortgage contracts. They are increasingly being enforced by lenders when buyers try to assume a seller's existing low-rate mortgage.

If your mortgage document includes a *due-on-sale clause*, the lender has the right to require immediate repayment of the unpaid balance if the property changes hands. Here is an example of a typical due-on-sale clause:

If all or any part of the Property or an interest therein is sold or transferred by the Borrower without the Lender's prior written consent . . . the Lender may, at the Lender's option, declare all the sums secured by this Mortgage to be immediately due and payable.

In due-on-sale cases, the courts frequently have upheld the lender's right to increase the interest rate to the prevailing market level.

Legal Tip: Be especially wary when a home seller offers to let you take over an "assumable mortgage." If the mortgage has a due-on-sale provision, the assumption may not be legal. If the deal goes through, the lender could raise the rate to the current market level, and you could be liable for a monthly mortgage payment hundreds of dollars higher than you planned.

You may be getting a loan that's more expensive than you can afford.

Annual Percentage Rate

Closing documents also can contain confusing information on interest rates.

When a home buyer applies for a mortgage and obtains a loan commitment, the federal Truth-in-Lending Act requires lenders to disclose the *annual percentage rate,* or the total charge for credit stated as a percentage, calculated on an annual basis.

APR allows different types of mortgages to be compared equally and fairly. On an adjustable-rate mortgage, APR equalizes such variables as rate adjustments, buydowns, first-year discounts, and other factors that affect the cost of an ARM.

Let's suppose you buy a $100,000 home, put $10,000 down and take out a $90,000 mortgage for 30 years at 10 percent interest. Your monthly principal and interest payment would be about $790.

However, in addition to this payment, the lender charges you 3 points—or $2,700—in closing costs. When these points are amortized over the life of the mortgage, your annual percentage rate on the loan actually is 10.37 percent, not 10 percent.

And, because your down payment is less than 20 percent, you are required to pay a private mortgage insurance premium of $450 the first year and a decreasing amount each year, beginning at about $300 until your equity in the house equals 20 percent.

PMI is considered part of APR. So, when those insurance premiums are added in, the interest rate on the loan jumps to 10.73 percent from 10.37 percent. In other words, a 10 percent nominal mortgage rate actually could be closer to 11 percent when APR is computed.

Disclosure Rules

The Truth-in-Lending Act and its implementing Regulation Z provide rules for consumer credit disclosures. Credit terms, including APR, must be printed "clearly and conspicuously" on the loan documents and in any advertisements.

If a mortgage seeker calls a lender on the telephone and asks for information regarding the cost of mortgage financing, the only rate the lender may legally give in response is the annual percentage rate.

Therefore, APR should be perfectly clear both to lenders and to borrowers. But it isn't. Depending on which savings and loan association, bank, or mortgage broker you talk to, some are eager to quote APR, and others aren't. Often, you will be quoted the annual interest and points separately.

"There isn't a conspiracy to withhold APR information from borrowers, but some loan officers do not compute it until the mortgage closes," said Chicago mortgage analyst Gary S. Meyers. "This is not a deceptive practice that the Federal Trade Commission should investigate. There is no plot to hide APR, and the Truth-in-Lending Act isn't being violated."

"The truth is some of today's home-loan programs are so complicated that many lenders simply do not know how to accurately calculate APR," Meyers added. "How do you compute the APR on an adjustable-rate mortgage when the interest rate is discounted in the first year?"

For example, one Chicago S&L offered a 7.75 percent first-year rate on an ARM. Because the loan has an annual cap, or limit, of 2 percentage points per year on rate adjustments, the lender projected the second-year rate at a maximum of 9.75 percent.

According to the mortgage document, the rate can go no higher than 13.5 percent during the 30-year term of the loan. Rate adjustments will be based on the movement of a cost of funds index for federally chartered S&Ls. So what's the APR? According to the computer, it is 10.216 percent.

Chances are your lender isn't sure what causes that rate to be the APR. And that means you probably won't.

"Don't ask me how to compute APR—there are 100 variables to consider," said Michael L. Allen, president of Crown Mortgage Company in Oak Lawn, Illinois. The firm has a computer hookup to the data bank of Mortgage Guaranty Insurance Corporation (MGIC), a private mortgage insurance company based in Milwaukee, Wisconsin.

"We tap into MGIC's computer via telephone. We feed mortgage data—the loan type, the interest charge, and other fees involved in computing APR—to MGIC through our terminal, and they give us the annual percentage rate in a printout. We pay a fee of $3 or $4 for each APR they compute."

Legal Tip: All lenders must use the same method of computing APR as defined by the Truth-in-Lending Act. So if the APR on your loan seems too high, ask the lender to recompute it.

As you can see, there can be many potential problems hidden in the fine print of mortgage documents. To blindly sign on the dotted line is the biggest mistake a novice borrower can make.

Even if you are a veteran of several real estate closings, experts recommend that you hire legal counsel to sort out confusing and unintelligible clauses found in most mortgage documents.

CHAPTER 8

THE 30-YEAR FIXED-RATE MORTGAGE

30-Year Fixed at a Glance

Interest rate: May be initially higher than other types of financing, but is fixed for the life of the loan.

Rate adjustments: None.

Payment changes: None.

Term of Loan: 30 years.

Maximum loan amount: $133,250, but lenders will make larger loans with slightly different terms.

Assumable: No.

Ideal for: First-time buyers.

If you are a home buyer shopping for a mortgage with stable monthly payments and long-term tax advantages, the 30-year fixed-rate loan may be ideal for your pocketbook.

ADVANTAGES

The 30-year fixed-rate mortgage has three notable advantages:

1. The biggest advantage is payment predictability.
2. There can be some hefty income tax write-offs in the early years of the loan, because the majority of early payments goes to interest charges.
3. Most lenders permit you to prepay the principal, allowing you to shorten effectively the term of the loan. But such prepayments are entirely up to you, because you are under no obligation to pay more than the monthly payments.

DISADVANTAGES

There are some disadvantages to consider as well:

1. Principal is paid down at a very slow rate, following the 30-year amortization schedule.
2. If you take out a loan at a high rate and interest rates fall, you will have the expense of refinancing if you want to take advantage of the lower rate.
3. If you sell your home, the buyer usually cannot assume the loan.
4. If you pay the loan off in less than 30 years, there may be a prepayment penalty.

STABLE MONTHLY PAYMENTS

The so-called old-fashioned 30-year fixed-rate loan originally was developed in the 1930s when long-term mortgages came into vogue.

The beauty of the 30-year fixed-rate loan is its stable monthly principal and interest payments. A home buyer who took out a $40,000, fixed-rate loan at 8 percent interest in the mid-1970s paid about $293 a month for principal and interest. Because of higher real estate taxes and insurance premiums, the monthly payment probably has increased, but the payment for principal and interest still is the same.

A few years ago, mortgage experts considered this type of loan a vanishing species because lenders had been burned by skyrocketing interest rates while they were holding older low-rate loans.

With long-term rates hovering near 16 percent, few borrowers could afford the payments required by a fixed-rate loan. Instead, they took adjustable-rate loans with low initial rates. As rates dropped in the mid-1980s, however, more borrowers qualified for 30-year fixed-rate loans and snapped them up.

The loan is popular because it eliminates the problem of "payment shock"—the unpleasant surprise to a family's budget caused by rate and payment increases—that can occur with adjustable-rate mortgages.

A 30-year, fixed-rate mortgage is set up so that the interest portion of each monthly payment decreases over time, while the principal portion increases. So, in the early years of the mortgage, the vast majority of your monthly payment goes for interest. All this interest is deductible from income in figuring your federal income tax. In the last few years of the loan, most of your payment is for principal, which is not deductible. The total payment, of course, remains the same.

When interest rates reach 11 or 12 percent, the 30-year fixed-rate loan tends to be more popular than its cousin, the 15-year fixed, because monthly payments are lower and more borrowers can qualify.

For example, the monthly principal and interest payment on a $90,000 mortgage at 10 percent for 30 years is $790. If you took out the same loan for 15 years, the payment would rise to $967—a difference of $177 a month, or enough to meet your car payment.

IDEAL FOR MIDDLE-INCOME FAMILIES

Because the monthly payments are lower than on most other loan options, 30-year fixed-rate loans are most popular with young, middle-income families who have the necessary down payment, but are trying to keep home expenses to a minimum.

You'll pay more interest on a 30-year loan than on the 15-year, but this is offset somewhat by the advantage of bigger tax deductions for mortgage interest. Also, equity buildup is slow with this type of loan.

For example, after 5 years of a 30-year loan at 10 percent interest, $966 of every $1,000 borrowed would still be owed. On a $90,000 loan, that means you still would owe $88,920. After 10 years, $909 of every $1,000 borrowed would still be owed—or $81,810 of that $90,000 loan. And, after 15 years, you'd still owe $817 of every $1,000 borrowed, or $73,530 of the $90,000 loan.

On a 15-year loan at 10 percent, after 5 years you'd owe $813 for every $1,000 borrowed, or $73,170 of the $90,000 loan. However, after 10 years, you would owe only $506 of each $1,000 borrowed, or $45,540, and after 15 years you'd own the home outright.

Although the fixed-rate loan has higher initial interest charges than the initial rate on many adjustable mortgages, it lets the borrower know exactly how much home-loan payments will be for the next 180 or 360 months.

Payments on adjustable-rate loans, or ARMs, can rise and fall with market conditions, leaving a homeowner guessing and worrying what his or her monthly housing expense will be. ARMs are discussed in detail in Chapter 14.

While the general characteristics of 30-year fixed-rate mortgages are the same, slightly different variations are offered by S&Ls, banks, and mortgage companies.

In choosing among the various offerings, the borrowers should first consider their down payment. The conventional fixed-rate mortgage generally requires a down payment of at least 5 percent, though some lenders increasingly are asking 10 percent down, and 20 percent is preferred. If the down payment is less than 20 percent, private mortgage insurance is required.

The Federal Housing Administration–insured fixed-rate mortgages allow a down payment of as little as 5 percent. Eligible veterans can obtain a Veterans Administration–guaranteed loan with no money down. FHA and VA loans will be covered in detail in Chapters 11 and 12.

LOAN MAXIMUMS VARY

If you take out a 30-year fixed at an S&L, bank, or mortgage company, your conventional fixed-rate loan probably will have a maximum amount of $133,250. That maximum is set by securities dealers who pool the loans into mortgage-backed securities, which are sold in the secondary mortgage market.

If you're moving to a dream home and hunting for a loan larger than $133,250, most S&Ls, banks, and mortgage companies offer a jumbo conventional loan. Amounts of $250,000 to $350,000 for 30 years at prevailing interest rates are fairly common. On occasion, even $1 million mortgages can be taken out. Unfortunately, most of us don't have to worry about such loans. Minimum down payments usually are 10 percent to 20 percent of the price.

CHAPTER 9

THE 15-YEAR LOAN: A SHORTCUT TO HOME OWNERSHIP

15-Year Fixed at a Glance

Interest rate: Fixed for the life of the loan and lower than on a 30-year fixed-rate mortgage.
Rate adjustments: None.
Payment changes: None.
Term of Loan: 15 years.
Maximum loan amount: $133,250, but lenders will make larger loans with slightly different terms.
Assumable: No.
Ideal for: Financially established second- and third-home buyers who expect to stay in their house at least 5 years.

If you expect to stay in your house at least 5 years, and if you can afford the higher monthly payments, you'll save tens of thousands of dollars in interest with a 15-

year mortgage rather than one for 30 years. And you will own your home completely in half the time it takes with a 30-year loan.

ADVANTAGES

Advantages of a 15-year fixed-rate loan include:

1. Monthly payments are fixed and predictable.
2. You'll get hefty interest savings over the life of the loan.
3. Rates can be 0.25 to 0.5 percentage point lower than on 30-year mortgages.
4. Equity in the home builds more quickly than with a 30-year loan.

DISADVANTAGES

You'll have to weigh at least two disadvantages:

1. Expect to make a larger monthly payment than on a 30-year loan. However, you may be surprised how little more it will be.
2. You'll need a larger annual income to qualify for the larger monthly payments; therefore you won't be able to purchase as expensive a home as you could with a 30-year loan.

FASTER PRINCIPAL PAYOFF

The 15-year loan is set up so that your home will be paid off in 180 equal monthly payments. The payment amount for principal and interest will remain the same over the course of the loan.

As with all mortgages, the majority of each payment is for interest for more than half of the loan's term. On a 15-year mortgage, however, a relatively substantial portion of the payment pays off the principal.

Today's lower interest rates are prompting more homeowners to consider a 15-year fixed-rate mortgage rather than the conventional 30-year mortgage.

In August 1985, the Mortgage Bankers Association of America reported that 1 in 7, or about 14 percent, of the home mortgages written for the previous 12 months were 15-year fixed-rate loans.

"That figure is really substantial when you consider at the beginning of 1983 the percentage of 15-year loans across the country was practically zero," said Thomas O. Marder, an MBA spokesman.

Marder said 15-year mortgages began gaining popularity in 1984 when the interest rates dropped below 13 percent and borrowers realized how little the difference in payments is between 15-year and 30-year loans.

"People think their payments will double with the 15-year loan. But what they don't realize is most of their payments in the beginning of either loan go to pay interest and very little actually goes toward the principal," said Karl Reinlein, senior vice president and regional manager of GMAC Mortgage Corp. in St. Louis.

Although payments are higher on the 15-year mortgage, interest rates and points tend to be slightly less than on the 30-year loan. There is also faster equity buildup and quicker payoff of the loan. Middle-aged homeowners prefer 15-year mortgages because they have higher income and want their house to be paid off before retirement. Also, some ambitious young people who want to be rid of a mortgage quickly prefer to build up equity for their next home on the 15-year loan.

To determine equity growth, refer to the loan progress charts in the Appendix.

HOW INTEREST IS SAVED

Most of the savings on the 15-year mortgage come

from the accelerated repayment of the principal, though the lower interest rates help, too.

Because each month's interest is figured on the unpaid principal balance, every dollar paid on principal reduces the interest payment for the next month and every month after that. So, the extra payment toward principal of a 15-year loan lowers each month's interest portion of your payment, leaving more for principal. Clearly, this effect snowballs—in your favor.

When you compare monthly payments and total interest charges on a $100,000 mortgage for 30 and 15 years, the difference is dramatic.

Let's suppose your brother-in-law took out a 30-year loan at 10.75 percent. The monthly principal and interest payment would be $933.48.

If you borrowed the same amount for 15 years at 10.25 percent, the monthly payment would be $1,089.95. You would be paying $156.47 a month more than the 30-year loan, but this entire amount would pay off the principal. You also benefit by the 0.5 percentage point lower interest rate on the 15-year loan.

After 5 years of the 30-year loan, your brother-in-law would still owe $970 for every $1,000 borrowed, or $97,000 of the $100,000 loan. After 10 years, he would still owe $919 of every $1,000 borrowed, or $91,900.

Meanwhile, after 5 years of your 15-year loan, you'd owe $816 of every $1,000 you borrowed, or $81,600 of the $100,000 loan. However, after 10 years, you would owe only $510 of every $1,000 borrowed, or $51,000. After 15 years, you'd be hosting a mortgage-burning party, while your brother-in-law still would owe $83,300—*more than 90 percent of the original loan amount.* He would continue paying $11,201.78 each year for another 15 years.

But, your brother-in-law says, "I saved $156.47 every month." If he invested that difference and earned 7 percent, compounded annually, in 15 years it would grow to nearly $50,000. You'll save that much in the first 5 years after the mortgage-burning party, although inflation may reduce the value of this savings somewhat.

Comparison of Payments

The following chart shows the monthly principal and interest payments for a 30-year and a 15-year fixed-rate mortgage for $50,000. You may be surprised at the difference. Also, remember that you often can obtain a lower interest rate on a 15-year loan than on a 30-year loan.

Interest Rate	15-Year Loan	30-Year Loan
8.0%	$ 9.56	$ 7.34
8.0%	$477.83	$366.89
8.5	492.37	384.46
9.0	507.14	402.08
9.5	522.12	420.43
10.0	537.31	438.79
10.5	552.70	457.37
11.0	568.30	476.17
11.5	584.10	495.15
12.0	600.09	514.31
12.5	616.27	533.63
13.0	632.63	553.10
13.5	649.16	572.71
14.0	665.88	592.44
14.5	682.76	612.28
15.0	699.80	632.23

DRAWBACKS OF
THE 15-YEAR MORTGAGE

While the 15-year loan is growing in popularity, it has some drawbacks.

Since the 15-year loan increases the amount of monthly payments, Reinlein pointed out that it limits the price range of a prospective home buyer.

"This loan is not for everyone because it definitely limits the amount of home you can buy," he said. "The typical person applying for a 15-year loan is someone who's owned a home before—someone who has a little discretionary income. It's not [usually] a loan for a newly married couple buying their first home. But it's a great loan and you build up equity fast. It just limits the amount of home you can buy."

The larger payments also are locked in, forcing you to pay that much. During hard times in the family budget, the larger payment may be a substantial drain. If you were voluntarily prepaying principal on a 30-year loan, however, you could stop doing so for a while without any problem.

CHAPTER 10

THE BIWEEKLY MORTGAGE: FOR YUPPIES ONLY

Biweekly Mortgage at a Glance

Interest rate: Lower than a 30-year mortgage and fixed for the life of the loan.
Rate adjustments: None.
Payment changes: None.
Term of Loan: 15–19 years.
Maximum loan amount: $133,250, but lenders will make larger loans with slightly different terms.
Assumable: No.
Ideal for: Young professionals with high income.

The biweekly loan, nicknamed the "Yuppie mortgage," is a relatively new type of home financing that can save the borrower a lot in interest payments.

Under the biweekly plan, principal and interest

payments are set up as if the loan were for 30 years. But instead of paying once a month, you make one-half of the monthly payment every 2 weeks. Many borrowers find this more closely matches their paychecks anyway.

There are 26 payments each year—or the equivalent of 13 monthly payments every year rather than the usual 12. The extra money goes to pay down the principal of the loan—fast—and the process is relatively painless. Making what amounts to an extra payment a year may not sound like much of a change, but its effect in cutting the time and cost of any mortgage is astounding.

ADVANTAGES

The biweekly mortgage has three major advantages:
1. You get hefty savings on interest payments.
2. Equity builds up fast.
3. The mortgage principal is paid off at a rate almost twice that of a conventional 30-year mortgage.

DISADVANTAGES

Some disadvantages of biweekly mortgages include the following:
1. Mortgage payments are more frequent, and total yearly payments are larger than on 30-year loans.
2. Higher payments could lower the maximum loan amount if normal underwriting ratios are used.
3. You get smaller tax deductions for mortgage interest.
4. There are potential loan servicing problems.

HOW A BIWEEKLY MORTGAGE WORKS

The greater frequency of mortgage payments speeds up the loan payoff. That's because the portion of each payment that goes for interest is determined by the amount of unpaid principal. If you make payments every 14 days rather than every 30 or 31, the principal—and resulting interest charge—is lowered more quickly. The difference may be a dollar or two at first, but it grows quickly. Also, the equivalent of one extra monthly mortgage payment also reduces principal—and the following interest charges—dramatically.

POPULAR ON THE EAST COAST

The idea for making mortgage payments every two weeks began in Canada. Originally, the biweekly mortgage was set up as an adjustable-rate loan. One early adjustable plan, introduced by the First National Bank of Elgin, Illinois, was touted by lenders as "a way to reduce the loan maturity period and overall interest expense by as much as 30 percent." The idea of biweekly payments attracted hundreds of calls, but the adjustability of the loan scared most of them away.

However, the biweekly mortgage really caught on when several East Coast lenders offered the program with a fixed interest rate. Now, this relatively new fixed-rate mortgage alternative is becoming popular with young urban professionals—or Yuppies—who live by electronic banking and credit cards.

Although the biweekly mortgage is not widely available, experts predict a promising future for the loan because more and more Americans are beginning to realize the dramatic interest savings they can reap on shorter-term mortgages.

Part of the new awareness came because of the growing acceptance of the 15-year fixed-rate mortgage. So many Americans are choosing the 15-year home loan that some lenders now consider it the "normal" fixed-rate mortgage.

Sunrise Federal Savings & Loan of Farmingdale, New York, unveiled a fixed-rate biweekly mortgage program that requires borrowers to make 26 payments a year—or one every 14 days. Each payment is exactly half of the equivalent 30-year monthly payment. The loan plan allows borrowers to pay off 30-year mortgages in just 17.6 years.

"Only a handful of banks and S&Ls in the U.S. are trying this, but our response has been phenomenal," said Joseph Melillo, a senior vice president at Sunrise Federal.

Sunrise Federal requires that borrowers open a NOW account offered by the S&L. Every 14 days, the mortgage payment is automatically withdrawn from the borrower's account. All money in the account earns 5.25 percent interest.

Another East Coast lender, Johnstown Savings Bank in Johnstown, Pennsylvania, said 80 percent of its mortgage business is on a biweekly basis. "Our home-loan business has doubled since introducing the Yuppie mortgage," said John Khuri, head of marketing at the bank.

CHALLENGES AND OPPORTUNITIES

"The new loan program represents a challenge as well as opportunities," said Doug Gallagher, president of Gallagher Financial Systems, a Coral Gables, Florida–based mortgage computer software firm.

Gallagher said the new biweekly mortgage does have some distinct advantages, but it also has disadvantages.

On a typical Yuppie mortgage, the borrower would make 495 biweekly payments, and the loan would be paid off in 19 years. When compared to the 360 payments necessary to pay off a 30-year loan, the Yuppie borrower would cut his interest payments nearly in half.

The 19-year payoff on the mortgage also results in rapid net equity accumulation, and generally the borrower will pay a lower interest rate and lower loan fees, Gallagher said.

Experts say the faster payments on a Yuppie mortgage also are a form of forced savings. A young couple who buy a house with a Yuppie mortgage, then have a family, will have equity on tap—ready to be borrowed just when their children reach college age.

A quick-payment mortgage also makes sense for middle-aged home buyers who want to own their house free and clear by the time they retire.

However, there are some disadvantages, too. "The borrower may not like the increased total yearly payments required for housing," said Gallagher. "It may result in a slightly lower maximum loan amount when normal underwriting ratios are figured on a biweekly loan.

"Furthermore, the borrower may not like the reduction in interest and its effect on income tax deductions. It also may be more difficult to qualify for a Yuppie mortgage.

"Another big disadvantage is the potential loan servicing nightmare—26 mortgage payments to collect each year, instead of 12," said Gallagher. And writing and keeping track of all those mortgage checks is a bookkeeping chore for the borrower.

Experts say lenders have not developed the computer software to handle the biweekly program. And the recent crush of mortgage applications caused by lower rates meant they had no incentive to try to increase business. Many lenders could barely handle the business they had.

However, Gallagher said some of the hassle can be eliminated if the biweekly payments are deducted automatically from an account with the lender.

Borrowers who are eager to start their own do-it-yourself version of the Yuppie mortgage can do so by paying extra each month toward their mortgage principal. An extra $50 or $100 paid each month will knock years off your mortgage and drastically reduce total interest charges. Principal prepayment will be discussed further in Chapter 17.

CHAPTER 11

FHA LOANS: HOW UNCLE SAM HELPS CASH-STRAPPED BORROWERS

FHA 203(B) Loan at a Glance

Interest rate: Fixed for the life of the loan. Sometimes lower than for conventional mortgages.
Rate adjustments: None.
Payment changes: None.
Term of Loan: 15 or 30 years.
Maximum loan amount: $67,500 to $90,000, depending on the loan.
Assumable: Yes.
Ideal for: Young buyers with stable or slowly increasing income but relatively little savings.

The Federal Housing Administration (FHA) insures up to 20 percent of all home loans originated in the United States. These loans are extremely popular among young home buyers who are short on down payment cash but have solid monthly income.

FHA loans are particularly attractive because they require a lower minimum down payment. In addition, government-backed loans are fully assumable with no prepayment penalties.

However, applications are tedious, and it may take months for the FHA to process the loan. In 1986, long delays for FHA appraisals and other paperwork caused an average processing time of 90 days.

In 1985 and 1986, a heavy influx of applications for FHA financing—including refinancing requests— caused the government agency to exhaust its credit authority, creating a loan logjam. Since autumn of 1985, Congress has granted FHA a series of short extensions of its statutory authority.

ADVANTAGES

FHA loans have a number of advantages:

1. Down payments are low. The minimum is 3 percent of the first $25,000 of *appraised value* plus 5 percent of the value over $25,000.
2. The loan is assumable by the home's next buyer.
3. There is no prepayment penalty.
4. Closing costs can be financed into the loan.

DISADVANTAGES

The negatives of FHA loans include the following:

1. Red tape and application delays are common.
2. High closing costs, a loan origination fee, and discount points are possible. Because interest rates on FHA loans usually are the lowest available in the marketplace, lenders often charge higher points than for conventional loans to make their

usual profit. However, points can be split by buyer and seller, and the purchaser can finance his or her share.

3. There is a maximum mortgage amount. Limits range from $67,500 to $90,000 depending on location.

GOVERNMENT INSURANCE

The Federal Housing Administration provides government insurance for home loans. The FHA administers the insurance part of the programs, and mortgage bankers and other private lenders provide the money.

By insuring the loans, the FHA protects lenders and makes them more willing to lend to home buyers. Lenders are willing to lend to less-affluent borrowers if the federal government is helping to reduce the risk. But the borrower has to pay a price.

If the lender is qualified for the FHA coinsurance program, the government mortgage insurance premium is 0.5 percentage point added to the interest rate. So, a 10.25 percent FHA loan really becomes a 10.75 percent mortgage.

If the lender is not a member of the coinsurance program, the borrower must pay only a one-time insurance premium of 3.8 percent of the loan amount at closing. This puts extra pressure on your down payment nest egg. If you stay in the house a number of years, the two programs probably would cost you the same amount. If you plan to stay just a few years, avoid the one-time premium.

Before approving a loan, the FHA will appraise the house to determine its fair market value. It also will inspect the house to make sure it meets basic structural requirements. If a home doesn't measure up, the seller will have to make repairs and pay for them before the FHA gives the green light.

There are several types of FHA loans, including

fixed-rate and graduated-payment loans. This chapter will focus on the fixed-rate FHA 203(B) loan. Graduated-payment loans will be covered in Chapter 15.

LOW DOWN PAYMENT

House hunters who qualify for an FHA-insured mortgage can buy a $60,000 home with a down payment of as little as $2,500, or 4.17 percent of the purchase price. (That's 3 percent of the first $25,000, or $750, plus 5 percent of the next $35,000, or $1,750, for a total of $2,500.)

The FHA 203(B) mortgage features a fixed, long-term interest rate. FHA rates no longer are set by the federal government—as they were until earlier this decade—but rise and fall depending on market conditions. The loans are available for 15 or 30 years. The interest rate on the 15-year variety generally is about 0.5 percentage points less than on the 30-year loan, reflecting the lower interest-rate risk the lender has on a shorter mortgage.

CLOSING FEES

On FHA loans, borrowers also are required to pay a loan origination fee of 1 percent of the mortgage amount. Many other types of loans do not require such a fee. Then there's another 1 percent for such closing costs as title insurance premium, survey, title search, mortgage recording, and other fees.

While these are substantial expenses, an FHA loan—unlike most other loans—allows the buyer to finance most of the closing costs. Allowable closing costs include the origination fee, mortgage insurance premium, title insurance policy, escrow fees, recording fees, and credit report. But be careful; these items must be added to the sale price before calculating the maximum FHA loan amount. Adding the fees to the loan amount reduces the cost of the home you can afford. And you will take 15 or 30 years to finally pay off the fees.

The FHA also allows the home seller and buyer to split discount points instead of forcing sellers to pay the whole amount and watch some of their profit go down the drain. Without the split, many sellers simply wouldn't sell to FHA borrowers.

In busy real estate markets, some sellers simply tack the points onto the price of the home or refuse to reduce the asking price for FHA borrowers while doing so for borrowers with conventional financing.

Discount points are special fees that lenders charge to increase their yield on these loans. A point equals 1 percent of the loan amount. Depending on market conditions, points can be from 1 percent to 8 percent of the loan amount, but most often they are in the range of 3 percent to 6 percent.

TOUGH FHA CREDIT STANDARDS

To limit the risk and probability of foreclosure or collection difficulties, the FHA uses tough credit standards in evaluating applicants.

"We review the borrower's financial history to make sure he can meet the mortgage payments and still have enough cash left over to live a decent life," said David Podbelski, chief of mortgage credit at the Chicago office of the Department of Housing and Urban Development. After all, both the lender and the borrower lose out if a borrower is in over his or her head.

There are no maximum income limitations on FHA home loans; they are open to all who can qualify. A good credit history is one of the principal considerations, Podbelski said.

In applying for an FHA loan, a borrower must meet the following criteria (which are similar to the standards lenders use on all loans):

Good credit history. FHA loan examiners depend heavily on information gathered by a reputable credit bureau about the borrower's previous record of financial responsibility.

"The loan examiner wants to know how the borrower manages his financial affairs," Podbelski said. "Uncle Sam believes past performance is the most reliable guide in determining the borrower's future credit behavior."

Usually at least two years of good credit history are required, unless the borrower is from a foreign country, has recently graduated from college or technical school, or has recently been discharged from the military service.

Income stability. Loan examiners look at employment information, an estimate of after-tax income, and details of financial obligations, such as credit card debt and other bills. The FHA credit examiner analyzes the borrower's income to determine whether it can be expected to continue through the first five years of the mortgage—the critical period during which most defaults occur.

Adequate assets. Borrowers also must prove they have enough cash to cover the down payment and points, closing costs, origination fees, and mortgage insurance premium, if they are not included in the mortgage amount.

In analyzing the borrower's credit record, Uncle Sam—like most lenders—does not blackball a borrower for an isolated case of unsatisfactory or slow payment of a debt or account. Instead, what counts is the general pattern of credit behavior.

CHAPTER 12

HOW VETERANS CAN BUY WITH LITTLE OR NO MONEY DOWN

VA Loan at a Glance

Interest rate: Maximum rate set by the Veterans Administration. Fixed rate for the life of the loan, usually slightly below market rates.

Rate adjustments: None.

Payment changes: None.

Term of Loan: 15 or 30 years.

Maximum loan amount: $110,000 with no down payment; $135,000 with down payment of 25 percent of the difference between $110,000 and loan amount.

Assumable: Yes.

Ideal for: U.S. armed services veterans who are buying their first home and are short on down payment cash; veterans moving up to a larger home who want to take advantage of benefits they have earned.

Veterans of U.S. military service who want to buy a home haven't been forgotten by Uncle Sam or America's mortgage lenders.

Every year, nearly 200,000 veterans finance the purchase of houses—or refinance their homes—with Veterans Administration-guaranteed mortgages. The VA program, begun in 1944 to help World War II veterans achieve the American dream of home ownership, backed 178,931 home loans totaling $11.4 billion in the 1985 fiscal year, which ended September 30, 1985.

In early 1986, when the maximum interest rate on VA mortgages declined to 9.5 percent from 10.5 percent, this loan was one of the best home-financing deals available in the United States. The VA rate hadn't dipped below 10 percent since April 22, 1979, when it was also 9.5 percent. The rate peaked at 17.5 percent in 1981.

Much like the FHA lending program, the VA loan plan was buried in a paper blizzard in early 1986, and it almost was shut down because the $11.5 billion in loan guarantees budgeted for fiscal 1986 were used up.

Congress expanded the budget to $18.2 billion to carry the program through fiscal 1986. However, the Office of Management and Budget has recommended that the loan origination fee be doubled to 2 percent from the current 1 percent, meaning veterans will have to pay more for this benefit.

ADVANTAGES

Following are some advantages of VA loans:

1. VA loans require no money down or a small down payment.
2. Payments for principal and interest are predictable because the interest rate remains constant over the life of the loan.
3. The loan can be assumed by the home's next

buyer. (If it is, the seller cannot take out another VA loan until this one is paid off.)

4. There is no prepayment penalty.

DISADVANTAGES

VA loans have a few disadvantages, too, including the following:

1. There are red tape and application delays, but not as bad as with FHA loans.
2. Because the government sets the interest rate, lenders may charge extra fees to bring the yield on the loan up to the level of other investments.

WHO IS ELIGIBLE FOR A VA LOAN?

Nearly 30 million veterans and spouses of deceased veterans are eligible for 15- and 30-year fixed-rate Veterans Administration–guaranteed mortgages that allow the purchase of a home with no money down.

The borrower must be an honorably discharged military veteran with 90 days of service during wartime or 181 days during peacetime. Men and women who entered the service after September 7, 1980, and who have been honorably discharged, must have served 24 months to be eligible.

Also eligible are unmarried surviving spouses of military personnel who died in service or from a service-related disability, and spouses of service members who have been captured or listed as missing in action.

Millions of veterans whose previous loans have been paid in full are eligible for new loans guaranteed by the Veterans Administration. If a veteran sells a home purchased with a VA mortgage, he or she can get another VA loan once the first is paid off.

If a vet sells to another veteran who is eligible, the

purchaser's entitlement can be transferred to the seller. The seller then may buy another house using the buyer's entitlement.

Also, if a veteran still has partial eligibility, he or she may buy a second home without selling the first one. Specifics about partial eligibility are available from the Veterans Administration.

TERMS OF A VA LOAN

Under current VA loan guarantees, eligible veterans have a $27,500 housing entitlement, which means they can borrow up to $110,000 for the purchase of a single-family home or a two- to four-unit apartment building with no money down.

The VA requires a down payment of 25 percent of the loan amount above $110,000, up to a maximum of $135,000. So, a down payment of $6,250 is required on the maximum loan.

Of course, VA borrowers face the usual credit evaluation and must be able to repay the loan. They also must live in the building being financed.

Vets also can use a VA loan to finance the purchase of a condominium or a mobile home, with or without a lot. The funding can be used to construct, rehab, repair, or refinance a home.

Veteran buyers can buy an apartment building with other vets and develop their own co-op housing. They can use part of the loan to pay for their own labor and materials to upgrade their living units.

VA LOAN FEES

The no-down-payment provision encourages irresponsible buyers to walk away from a home when finances become too much, leaving the VA to help pay off the lender. This depletes VA resources.

So, the Office of Management and Budget in 1984

recommended dropping the no-down-payment provision in favor of a minimum 5 percent down payment. There has been no push, however, for immediate enforcement.

The buyer pays a total of 3 points on a VA loan. Borrowers must pay a loan origination fee of 1 percent of the mortgage amount. Closing costs are 1 percent for title insurance premium, survey, title search, mortgage recording, and other fees. The VA also charges a 1 percent loan guarantee fee, which can be added to the mortgage amount. This money is funneled into the VA loan guarantee fund to help make the program more self-sufficient. This revolving fund is used to pay off lenders' claims resulting from foreclosure.

Because the VA loan rate is set by Uncle Sam and usually is slightly below market rates, lenders charge points ranging from 2 to 6 percent of the loan amount to increase their yield. Under VA regulations, these points must be paid by the seller and not packed into the price of the house.

Sometimes, however, it's hard to ensure that this is true. After all, why would the seller want to lose 6 percent of his or her profit by selling to a VA borrower rather than a conventional borrower?

If you are a veteran who has not taken advantage of your VA-guaranteed loan benefits, check with your local VA office for details, or contact the Veterans Administration, Washington, D.C. 20420.

CHAPTER 13

MORTGAGE BOND FINANCING: POPULAR AND ENDANGERED

> *Mortgage Bond Loans at a Glance*
>
> *Interest rate:* Usually 2 or 3 percentage points below market rates.
> *Rate adjustment:* None.
> *Payment changes:* None.
> *Term of Loan:* 30 years.
> *Mortgage amount:* Any amount for homes costing up to 10 percent above the median-priced home in the local community.
> *Assumable:* No.
> *Ideal for:* First-time home buyers.

In the last decade and a half, 49 states have issued billions of dollars worth of tax-exempt bonds to make fixed-rate home loans available for first-time buyers at below-market rates. In the 50th state, Kansas, local governments issue bonds.

Under these programs, families with annual incomes as low as $20,000 can purchase new or resale homes. Usually rates are 2 or 3 percentage points lower than the conventional mortgage rate, depending on the bond market.

ADVANTAGES

Among the advantages of mortgage bond financing are the following:

1. Interest rates are substantially below market rates.
2. Down payment requirements are low.
3. Borrower income requirements are easier to meet.
4. Rates and payments for principal and interest are fixed for the length of the mortgage.

DISADVANTAGES

There are two main disadvantages:

1. Only first-time buyers—and sometimes other buyers in depressed areas—are eligible.
2. Because of heavy demand, these loans often are distributed by lottery. So, borrowers often have to be both needy and lucky.

HOW ONE BOND PLAN WORKS

When mortgage rates ranged from 12.25 percent to 13.5 percent in early 1985, first-time home buyers in Illinois obtained 30-year fixed-rate loans at 10.78 percent through a state mortgage-bond plan.

A lottery, administered by the Illinois Housing Development Authority, allocated $130 million for mortgages for borrowers who earned no more than $52,000 a year.

The state also set the maximum purchase prices of the eligible single-family homes, condominiums, and two- to four-unit apartments. Tax-exempt bond financing cannot be used for homes costing more than 10 percent above the median-priced home in the local community. Also, at least 20 percent of the money raised through the bond sale must be used in economically distressed neighborhoods.

Illinois also required that the borrower hadn't owned a home in the previous 3 years—its definition of a first-time buyer. Borrowers also had to pay a loan origination fee of 1 percent of the loan amount.

WHY THE RATES ARE LOWER

The money for these programs is raised by selling bonds to investors. Because these bonds meet U.S. requirements, the interest paid to the investors is free from federal income taxes. Because investors don't lose a substantial portion of their interest income to Uncle Sam, they are willing to accept a lower interest rate. The lower interest rate is then passed along to borrowers.

U.S. TREASURY OPPOSITION

Despite these programs' popularity with borrowers, state and local governments, and the housing industry, this type of financing has come under fire from the federal government.

The Reagan administration worried about the loss of federal revenue. In 1981 and 1982—two of the biggest years for tax-exempt mortgage revenue bonds since states began participating in 1970—the financing programs cost the federal government more than $2.6

billion in lost revenue, according to the Government Accounting Office.

For that reason, Congress has restricted use of the program to single-family homes for first-time buyers and placed a cap on the volume of bonds a state and all of its localities may issue.

Housing finance officials say mortgage bond financing is the only way many moderate-income home buyers can afford the American Dream.

"We're not in business to compete with banks," said Robert Sonnek of the Minnesota Housing Finance Agency. "Because of the tax exemption, we can provide a product banks cannot provide." He added that without a program aiding families who cannot afford conventional mortgage rates, "there is no way you're going to get those people into houses."

Only time will tell whether such programs can survive the ever-searching cleaver of federal budget cuts.

CHAPTER 14

ADJUSTABLE-RATE MORTGAGES: A CHANGE IN THE RULES

ARMs at a Glance

Interest rate: Initially about 2 percentage points lower than a conventional fixed-rate loan; in the second period may be comparable to a fixed-rate mortgage.

Rate adjustment: Usually every one, three, or five years, depending on the mortgage. Most loans limit how much the rate can change each period and over the length of the loan.

Payment changes: Can change as often as rates can, so every one, three, or five years.

Term of Loan: 30 years.

Assumable: Yes.

Ideal for: White-collar workers who expect to be transferred within three years and other borrowers who have the financial means to handle increased payments, but expect interest rates to decline.

Mortgage lenders love adjustable-rate home loans. That's probably the biggest reason home buyers should be wary of them, consumer advocates say.

Getting a handle on how much a home buyer will pay over the life of an adjustable-rate mortgage (ARM) is like trying to grab hold of an eel. And the unwary borrower who chooses an ARM may feel wrapped in the embrace of an octopus. Eventually the borrower may be swimming in a sea of red ink.

ADVANTAGES

ARMs do have advantages. Following are the three major ones:

1. Below-market first-year payments make the first year (period) of home ownership easier to adjust to financially.
2. Consumers are protected by annual and life-of-loan rate and payment caps.
3. Borrowers can benefit from future interest-rate declines without the costs and hassles of refinancing.

DISADVANTAGES

In terms of disadvantages, you'll want to consider the following:

1. Rate and payment increases in second and subsequent years (periods) can shock the borrower's budget.
2. Negative amortization is possible.
3. The future cost of a home is impossible to know.

HOW ARMs WORK

ARMs allow lenders to change the borrower's interest rate, monthly payment, and/or principal balance based on shifts in economic indicators, or indexes. Lenders adjust the interest rate on the loan in regular prespecified intervals—usually every 1, 3, or 5 years—based on movements of the index. Lenders then add a profit margin of 2 to 2.5 percentage points to compute the new rate.

Typical indexes on which ARMs are adjusted include the one-year T-bill index, an average of U.S. securities yields, or the Federal Home Loan Bank Board's monthly Cost of Funds Index, which charts the average rates federally chartered S&Ls pay savers and other lenders.

Most banks and S&Ls would prefer borrowers to choose ARMs because the flexible rate protects the institution in times of inflation. Instead of being locked into fixed-rate obligations—as many S&Ls and banks were in the early 1980s—the financial institution can pass along to borrowers rate increases allowed under terms of the loan. This leaves the borrower, not the lender, at the mercy of rate charges.

A BAD REPUTATION

Adjustable mortgages got a bad reputation in the early 1980s when rates were high and still-evolving ARMs were the only type of financing many people could afford.

In 1983 and 1984, when fixed- rate loans were above 13 percent, it was not uncommon for lenders to quote a first-year ARM rate as low as 6 or 7 percent. Despite the first-year bargains, ARM borrowers found themselves paying close to the same rate as fixed mortgages when the loans were adjusted for the second year. And the mortgage agreement allowed the rate to go even higher if the index of rates did.

More recently, however, interest-rate and payment caps were added to protect borrowers. Even so, the amount of the monthly check the borrower sends the lender can change annually or every three or five years. That doesn't sit well with many borrowers.

In 1984 nearly two-thirds of the home-loan origination activity was in ARMs, compared to only 5 percent in 1981. However, in 1985, the share of ARM loan activity dropped to about 50 percent. With the decline of mortgage rates and the re-emergence of affordable fixed-rate loan alternatives, experts say ARMs lost momentum, but they probably will be a fixture in the future marketplace.

"Its share of the market may rise and fall depending on market interest rates, but the ARM has become a permanent feature of the mortgage market," said John B. Zellars, chairman of the U.S. League of Savings Institutions, a trade organization that represents the S&L industry.

Lenders also say ARMs keep mortgage money available during times of high interest rates. When interest rates—especially long-term fixed rates—rose in mid-1984, ARMs were available to borrowers. Few buyers would have—or could have—taken on fixed-rate loans at 15 percent.

ARMs START TO FADE

With rates on fixed mortgages down sharply since then, the tide of home-loan activity again is receding from ARMs.

"S&L-industry ARM volume is down sharply in recent months because the interest-rate spread between the 30-year fixed mortgage and the second year of an adjustable is less than 0.5 percentage point," said Eugene J. Rudnick, Jr., president of Peerless Federal Savings and Loan Association in Chicago. In the third and all subsequent years, the rate—and payments— could exceed the fixed rate.

ARM lending also has started to sink because

lenders are more nervous about a higher default ratio with ARMs than with fixed-rate instruments, as well as a growing number of foreclosures. In 1984, the Federal National Mortgage Association, which buys home loans from lenders, recently stopped buying ARMs from 3 mortgage companies and put 50 other firms on probation because of a high rate of borrower defaults.

Mortgage analysts say much of the ARM default and foreclosure activity resulted from abuses by lenders. To qualify the more hard-pressed buyers, lenders offered discounted ARMs for one year.

"Discounted to rates of 10, 9, 8 percent or below, ARMs were pep pills to the housing market," said mortgage banker James Wooten, president of Dallas-based Lomas & Nettleton.

The problem is that below-market introductory interest charges—called teaser rates—last only a year or two. In the second year, adjustment indexes click in and interest rates float—or sometimes splash loudly—toward market rates. Some consumers have been caught unprepared for the rapidly shifting tide of payments.

Worried that, like an iceberg, an ARM hides many of its vices, consumer advocates said these mortgages not only are confusing, they are dangerous. Rising interest rates could force mortgage payments so high that homeowners would become unable to afford the monthly payments in a year or two. The American Dream of home ownership and a borrower's good credit history would be obliterated by red ink.

STANDARDIZED ARM REQUIREMENTS

Finally in mid-1984, Congress put pressure on the mortgage industry to standardize ARMs. Today, some general requirements apply. (The first five requirements are no different from those used for 30-year fixed-rate loans.) These requirements are:

1. A borrower's first-year mortgage payment usually must be no more than 28 percent of his or her gross income.

2. The maximum loan amount generally is $133,250, though some savings and loans will lend as much as $500,000.

3. Monthly payments are based on a 30-year amortization schedule.

4. The minimum down payment is 5 percent, but most lenders now require 10 percent down.

5. If the down payment is less than 20 percent, private mortgage insurance will be required to protect the lender from default.

6. Generally, movements in the interest rates on capped adjustable mortgages are limited to 2 percentage points per year and 5 percentage points over the life of the loan.

7. Adjustable programs will limit negative amortization to 125 percent of the mortgage amount. (Negative amortization occurs if the interest rate on an ARM is adjusted upward and monthly payments do not cover interest charges. The interest owed is tacked onto the loan amount.)

ARM PLANS VARY

There are several ARM plans approved by the Federal National Mortgage Association and available at S&Ls, banks, and mortgage companies.

The most popular ARM program calls for annual interest-rate and payment adjustments. In mid-1986, depending on the lender originating the mortgage, first-year interest rates ranged from 7.75 percent to 9.9 percent. Lenders generally charge points, or closing costs, of 2 percent to 3 percent of the loan amount.

Although this plan currently is the most viable ARM

program, borrowers should shop for the best rates at S&Ls eager to peddle this loan. Be sure to ask the lender what index is used and what margin is added. Have the lender compute the second-year rate and payment based on today's index and the margin.

ARM SCENARIOS

One-Year ARM

Suppose you need a $90,000 home loan and take out a typical one-year ARM from your local savings and loan association. With a first-year rate of 8.5 percent amortized over 30 years, monthly principal and interest payments would be $692.

You'd also have to pay the usual closing costs, including 3 points—$2,700—and a $250 loan application fee. With a minimum down payment of 10 percent, private mortgage insurance would be required. There would be a first-year insurance premium of 0.5 percent of the loan amount—$450.

The second-year insurance fee would be 0.34 percent of the loan balance, or about $300 a year. Payable in monthly installments, that would increase your monthly payment to about $717.

Suppose future interest-rate adjustments are based on the Federal Home Loan Bank Board's Cost of Funds Index. Then, a 2.5 percentage-point margin for costs and profit is added to the index value.

If the index were at 10 percent after one year, the second-year rate on your ARM would be 12.5 percent (10 percent plus the 2.5 percentage-point margin). Your principal and interest payments would rise to about $945. The PMI would raise your total monthly payment to about $970 from $717. That's a payment jump of nearly 32 percent in the second year. No wonder consumerists worry about the payment shock of ARMs.

Five-Year ARM

Another ARM plan calls for rate adjustments once a year, but payment adjustments only every five years.

However, if the payment is insufficient to cover interest-rate increases, negative amortization will occur, and the loan balance automatically will be increased. If the payment is more than enough, the additional amount pays off principal. The possibility of negative amortization makes borrowers shy away.

Three-Year ARM

With another ARM, both the rate and monthly payment can be adjusted every three years. Regardless of where the index goes, the maximum increase on the rate is 2 percentage points per adjustment period, and 5 percentage points over the life of the loan, depending on the lender.

If you are planning to move to another house in 2 or 3 years, a bargain initial-rate ARM, say at 8.5 percent in the first year, might be a useful financing tool. For example, if the loan has a 2 percent annual cap, the rate can't rise to more than 10.5 percent at the beginning of the second year, regardless how high the appropriate index rises.

Also, borrowers who expect interest rates to decline can benefit from an ARM. Assume the same initial rate of 8.5 percent when fixed-rate loans are at 10.5 percent. If rates drop, the ARM borrower's rate may rise, but not at all near 10.5 percent, the fixed-rate choice. Of course, rates also can go up.

ARMs CAN BE CONVERTED

Many adjustable plans allow the borrower the option of converting an ARM to a fixed-rate loan on the anniversary of the adjustment period. This option was added to attract borrowers who wanted a fixed rate but couldn't afford it at the time the loan was made.

However, Michael L. Allen, president of Crown Mortgage Company in Oak Lawn, Illinois, advises borrowers to ask about the program's conversion factor.

If a borrower wants to convert to a fixed loan, some lenders will do so at the current market rate for fixed-rate loans plus a margin, usually 0.25 percentage point.

The ARM rate—either current or when you took the loan—has nothing to do with the fixed interest rate at conversion.

Despite vast improvements in ARMs to increase consumer protection, to the average borrower these lending programs still are about as clear as octopus ink. But the savings and loan industry is continuing to tout ARMs as the greatest invention since the life preserver.

"There has been so much negative publicity about ARMs that buyers are wary," Allen said. "What's happened is there's so much consumer protection, which caused tighter regulations, that fewer buyers are qualifying."

CHAPTER 15

GROWING-EQUITY LOANS AND OTHER INNOVATIVE MORTGAGES

GEM Loans at a Glance

Interest rate: Rate is fixed for entire length of the loan.
Rate adjustment: None.
Payment changes: In years 2 through 6, the monthly payment may increase annually, then level off.
Term of Loan: 13 to 17 years.
Assumable: No.
Ideal for: Upwardly mobile borrowers who expect their income to increase much faster than inflation.

Growing-equity mortgages are geared for borrowers who expect their income to increase substantially within a few years. On these loans, the monthly payments will increase annually to pay off the loan faster.

Much like a 15-year fixed-rate mortgage, the GEM is based on larger payments than on 30-year loans, faster equity growth, and a shorter mortgage term.

ADVANTAGES

The pluses to consider with the GEM are the following:

1. Equity grows rapidly through gradually increasing principal payments.
2. Total interest payments are less than on 30-year fixed-rate loans.
3. The first-year payment is below the market rate.

DISADVANTAGES

The minuses to consider are the following:

1. After the first year, payments generally are higher than on a 15-year fixed loan.
2. If income doesn't keep pace with rising monthly payments, the cost of home ownership may be prohibitive.

RISING INCOME NEEDED

Typically, monthly payments rise slightly each year—by 3 or 4 percent—with all the increased cash flow paying off the outstanding principal and giving the borrower more equity in the home. At the same time, the higher payments help decrease the length of the loan.

Lenders like GEMs because lenders collect the borrower's interest and principal payments faster through the accelerated cash flow and can reinvest them. This provides the lender more protection against inflation.

There are many variations on the GEM theme, but only two basic plans. One starts out with a rate and payments much like a 30-year fixed-rate mortgage, but the payments increase annually until the loan is paid off. The extra amount goes entirely toward principal, and the loan usually is paid off in 13 to 17 years. This choice is preferable for borrowers because they never lose equity.

Another widely used GEM involves artificially low payments in the early years, which cause the loan's principal balance to *increase* for a few years through negative amortization. Payments increase annually until year 6, when they level off. The increase in payments goes toward principal, helping to retire the loan early.

Only borrowers who are unable to make the necessary payments for the first variation of a GEM should look at this second choice. That's because there is negative amortization and the annual percentage rate on this loan usually is higher than a fixed-rate, level-payment, 15-year mortgage—a plan the GEM attempts to mimic.

Here's how this GEM would work. Let's assume the first-year monthly payment is based on an interest rate of 9.5 percent. In years 2 through 6, the monthly payment increases 7.5 percent. The rate on which the payment is based increases by 1 percentage point annually, leveling off at 14.5 percent and remaining there for the rest of the 15-year loan.

The annual percentage rate averages 13.78 percent over the life of the loan. That's a terrible deal, considering that today you can lock in a 15-year fixed-rate loan for a much, much lower rate. Also, because early-year payments are artificially low, a borrower will owe more upon sale after 3 years than upon the original closing.

The maximum loan amount under a GEM ranges from $133,250 to $300,000, and down payments run from 5 percent to 20 percent. Lenders also charge points and a loan application fee. If the down payment is less than 20 percent, private mortgage insurance is required.

GRADUATED-PAYMENT MORTGAGE

The graduated-payment mortgage (GPM) is designed primarily for young buyers on the way up—those who expect their income to increase steadily over the years. The loan is ideal for those who cannot afford higher payments now but whose potential indicates a higher income level in the near future.

GPM Loans at a Glance

Interest rate: Rate is fixed for entire length of the loan.

Rate adjustment: None.

Payment changes: Monthly payments start out low, increase gradually over the first five or 10 years of the loan, then level off. Payments are larger than a normal fixed-rate loan in the remaining years of the mortgage to repay the shortfall (negative amortization) in the early years.

Term of Loan: 30 years.

Assumable: No.

Ideal for: Young buyers who expect their income to increase steadily over the years.

The idea behind the GPM is to provide smaller-than-normal payments in the early years of the loan and larger-than-normal payments in the later years. Regulations regarding the GPM were incorporated into the National Housing Act of 1974. In 1977, the Federal Housing Administration introduced the FHA 245 program, a GPM loan that helped countless thousands of young buyers afford homes.

Monthly payments on a GPM start out lower than they would under a fixed-payment mortgage, but they will surpass a similar fixed-rate loan when they level off in 5 to 10 years.

Buyers opting for a GPM may choose from a varied menu of payment schedules. For example, for the first 5 years, payments could increase 2.5 percent, 5 percent, or 7.5 percent annually, then level off for the remaining years of the loan. Another option is annual payment increases of 2 percent for 10 years, then level payments until the loan is paid off.

If a borrower's income has not kept pace as expected, financial hardship and possible loss of the home could result. This is an extraordinarily serious drawback.

The second drawback to the GPM is negative amortization. Because the payments in the early years are less than the interest owed, the monthly shortfall is added to the unpaid balance. Typically, not a nickel of the principal on the original mortgage amount is paid off until nearly the 14th year on a 30-year mortgage.

You'll pay a great deal more interest on a GPM than on a similar conventional fixed-rate mortgage. You'll get a tax deduction, but for a person in the 28 percent tax bracket, the additional tax deductions are worth only 28 cents on the dollar.

If you sell your house after six or seven years, you'll owe more money than you did when you first took out the loan. This gives you less equity for purchasing another home.

SHARED-APPRECIATION MORTGAGE

With a shared-appreciation mortgage (SAM), the buyer gets a lower interest rate by agreeing to share part of the increased value of the property with the lender when the house is sold.

SAM Loans at a Glance

Interest rate: The rate can be significantly lower than conventional fixed mortgages. However, the borrower must share with the lender the home's increased value when the loan term expires or the house is sold.

Rate adjustment: None.

Payment changes: Monthly payments are fixed for the life of the loan.

Term of Loan: 10 years.

Assumable: No.

Ideal for: Borrowers with potential for higher income who want to buy a more expensive home now, but can't qualify for the monthly payments.

Typically, the lender would offer an interest rate about one-third lower than the prevailing market rate and in return receive one-third of the owner's appreciation when the home is sold. In effect, the lender becomes the homeowner's partner.

Let's suppose the going rate on a 30-year fixed mortgage is 15 percent, and you need a $90,000 loan. Monthly principal and interest payments would be

$1,138. But the lender offers you a SAM loan at 10 percent—and a monthly payment of $790. You save $348 a month, or $4,176 a year.

Seven years later, your $100,000 house is worth $142,000. One-third of that appreciation—$14,000— goes to the lender. It won't be fun writing that check.

And if you don't want to sell after 10 years, the usual length of a SAM, you may have to get the home appraised, pay the lender his or her share, and refinance the expired mortgage.

In addition, there are tax implications. You can deduct the lender's share of any appreciation from your federal income tax as interest.

Consumer groups have other concerns about SAMs. Who pays for improvements to the home? Should the lender pay one-third the cost of a room addition or a new roof? How about the homeowner's labor for maintaining the property?

Because interest rates are low and other mortgage financing is available, these questions are currently moot. Except during times of relatively high interest rates, no wise borrower will touch a SAM.

CHAPTER 16

MORTGAGES FOR THE ELDERLY

Grannie Maes at a Glance

Interest rate: Yield based on return on annuity.
Rate adjustment: None.
Payment changes: None.
Term of Loan: Depends on age of borrower.
Assumable: No.
Ideal for: Elderly borrowers who want to convert the equity in their house into cash but don't want to move.

Being house-rich and cash-poor is a dilemma for many of America's nearly 20 million elderly homeowners. Because a person's house is also his or her home, the elderly person often thinks of that asset as untouchable.

But the relatively golden retirement annuity mortgage, or "Grannie Mae," may be the pot of gold about which every retiree dreams.

ADVANTAGES

Some advantages of the Grannie Mae are these:

1. It allows an elderly homeowner to convert home equity into cash without being forced to move.
2. The borrower is guaranteed a life-long lease.
3. The investor gets a tax break by writing off maintenance, repairs, and depreciation on the income property.

DISADVANTAGES

The homeowner should consider at least three disadvantages:

1. The elderly homeowner must find an investor willing and financially able to handle the commitment.
2. The fair market rent may be too high for the borrower to pay.
3. Closing costs are higher than for a conventional loan.

SOLVING THE CASH FLOW PROBLEM

Grannie Mae involves the sale of a home to the owner's child or children. The buyer then rents the home back at fair market value. In addition, the parent receives a lifetime lease on the home and a monthly payment—for life—that is funded by the home's selling price.

Because the Grannie Mae requires the sale of the property to a child or group of children, the lender never is the landlord, nor can the lender ever evict the elderly resident. Instead, the lender's involvement is limited to issuing a mortgage for the child/investor.

Even if the children sell the home or the lender is forced to foreclose, the parent's lease continues.

The child or children get a tax break by writing off maintenance, repairs, and depreciation on the income property—expenses that wouldn't be deductible if the parent owned the home.

Often the home-buying child is in a higher tax bracket than the retired parent, so deductions for mortgage interest, property taxes, and other costs are more advantageous to the younger generation. The higher the child/investor's income tax bracket, the better the Grannie Mae works.

Annuity Pays the Rent

The monthly payment or annuity, resulting from the investment of the sale proceeds with an insurance company, pays the rent directly to the child/investor. Any amount more than the rent is paid directly to the elderly person for the rest of his or her life.

The annuity payment could be structured to increase at a predetermined rate every year to cover anticipated increases in rental costs—and to represent compounding of the principal amount.

Of course, an annuity payment that does not change will start out much higher than one that will increase. The amount of the annuity is based on the investment and the age and sex of the elderly resident(s).

An annuity for a 55-year-old man is structured to pay out for 22 years, the person's life expectancy. For a 55-year-old woman, it will pay out for 26 years. And for a 55-year-old couple, it will pay out for 30 years.

In contrast, the annuity is structured for just 6 years for an 85-year-old man, 8 years for an 85-year-old woman, and 9 years for an 85-year-old couple. Each payment would be larger for an 85-year-old than a 55-year-old.

If a 55-year-old man dies at 57, the balance is remitted to the estate. If, however, he lives until age 85, he will continue to receive the monthly payment until his death.

To see how Grannie Mae works, let's take the example of a $100,000 home sold to a child/investor by a 55-year-old widower. On the $100,000, there would be $4,200 in loan origination fees, and title insurance and closing costs would have to be paid, leaving $95,800 to invest in the annuity.

The selling widower would receive a monthly annuity of $772 for the rest of his life. In turn, the widower would pay $500 a month for rent and still have $272 from the home for other expenses. Of course, any pension and Social Security income would be additional.

There Are Drawbacks

Financial planners warn that, as with most innovative mortgages, Grannie Mae has disadvantages and may not be for everyone. Here are a few of the sticking points:

Negative Cash Flow for the Child/Investor. Although the child/investor receives the tax advantages of owning an investment property, the rental payments seldom cover the mortgage payments. That means such a plan requires monthly cash outlay.

Parental Allowance. Even with the annuity payment, pension, and Social Security, the parents may not have enough money for other living costs after paying a fair market rent. Supportive children may have to give money to their parents to help make ends meet.

Sibling Partnerships. If more than one child/investor

owns the house, various siblings may have different financial resources and different needs. What happens if the roof has to be replaced or if one child/investor needs cash for immediate expenses several years into a Grannie Mae?

Tax Liability. What happens if the parent dies and the child/investors haven't finished paying off the Grannie Mae? Such possibilities should be addressed in the parent's will. This is one excellent reason to use an attorney at the closing of the Grannie Mae.

Costly Fees. There is also a fee for the Grannie Mae. At the First National Bank of Chicago, for example, the usual fee for a mortgage is 3 points, but for the Grannie Mae the lender charges 4 points. Using the standardized Grannie Mae documents reduces the usual legal costs of setting up such a financial arrangement, but an attorney should be consulted before anything is signed. After all, you can be sure First National's attorneys have everything in the contract that *they* want.

The idea for Grannie Mae was developed by Kenneth Rosen, chairman of the real estate program at the University of California at Berkeley. Today, these loans are being offered by the Family Backed Mortgage Association, a for-profit group that is selling the mortgages to First National and a dozen other lenders that do business in all 50 states.

"With the Grannie Mae, an elderly person is not taking his total equity and gambling it away," said Richard Puntillo, president of Family Backed Mortgage Association.

Although only a few hundred Grannie Mae loans have been sold nationally, Puntillo said, the mortgage has 12 million to 15 million potential clients. "It's a new concept," he explained. "It takes time to convince people that it's doable and in their best interests."

REVERSE ANNUITY MORTGAGES

With the reverse annuity mortgage (RAM), there is no need for a family member to act as investor. The lender simply enters into an agreement with a homeowner regarding the equity in his or her home.

> ### RAMs at a Glance
>
> *Interest rate:* Yield is based on return on annuity.
> *Rate adjustment:* None.
> *Payment changes:* No.
> *Term of Loan:* 10 years.
> *Assumable:* No.
> *Ideal for:* Elderly persons who want to convert the equity on their house into cash, but don't want to move.

Under the RAM, the retired homeowner is paid regular monthly income based on an annuity drawn against the equity in the home. As the money is paid out, the principal borrowed each month continues to build up in the form of a larger loan balance.

The theory behind the reverse annuity mortgage is that retired homeowners would use up some or all of their home's equity while they are alive and thus be able to live more independently.

Reverse mortgages usually are based on a 10-year reverse term. At the end of the 10 years, the homeowner must repay the amount borrowed at the agreed-upon rate of interest in a prescribed period of time.

Because the interest from the RAM is accruing and compounding at the same time, the loan balance will grow exponentially as time passes. The idea is to pay off the loan eventually when the house is sold, supposedly after the elderly owner dies or no longer wants to live there.

However, critics say when the reverse annuity mortgage runs out, the lender is left with title to the property, and the former homeowner has neither a home nor equity.

The RAM concept was introduced in 1981 when the Federal Home Loan Bank Board authorized the nation's savings and loan associations to write them on an experimental basis. Only a few S&Ls have done so.

Lenders are urging that mortgage insurance be required to protect them against borrowers who outlive their loans. They don't want to be forced to evict an elderly person.

Clearly, for most elderly homeowners, this mortgage option is much less desirable than the Grannie Mae.

INDIVIDUAL RETIREMENT MORTGAGES

Another form of RAM, called the Individual Retirement Mortgage Account, allows the borrower to stay in the home the rest of his or her life.

The annuity payment is made at a fixed rate, often fairly low, and the homeowner agrees to pay the lender a percentage of the increase in the house's value over the term of the annuity.

If the home appreciates substantially in value, the lender benefits. Otherwise the borrower does better. Because the entire equity in the home is rarely at stake, the payments to the elderly homeowner are dramatically less than with a Grannie Mae.

This type of reverse annuity mortgage was developed in 1984 by Prudential-Bache Securities in New Jersey, where the company wrote 170 RAMs at 11.5 percent interest.

The homeowner must be age 62 or older. If the property is held in joint tenancy, the younger partner must be at least 62 years old.

The Annuity

Under the program, the borrower gets a lifetime annuity check that can range from a minimum of $100 a month to a maximum of $700. A lump sum cash advance also is possible.

The amount of the annuity is based on the home-owner's age, the home's market value, and the owner's equity in the property. The entire property need not be committed to the plan.

A fixed interest rate is charged on the cumulative outstanding balance. In addition, the lender pockets all of the appreciation in the value of the house, or its share of the increase if only part of the property is committed. No credit report, income statement, or financial records are required.

Repayments Not Required

The homeowner is never required to make any repayments during occupancy of the home or to leave the home. Nor will his or her heirs owe anything, even if the lender's payout vastly exceeds the house's value at the time of death.

The important thing to remember about RAMs is that these loans rapidly eat up the home equity it took decades to build.

"I advise senior citizens to be certain that they have other assets available if they are planning to go the reverse mortgage route," warned Deborah Ann Ford, professor of economics and finance at the University of Baltimore. "Otherwise, if they are forced to sell their homes eventually, they may not have the resources to live comfortably."

CHAPTER 17

CREATIVE FINANCING

Creative financing is a high-flying route to home ownership. It isn't weighted down by the baggage of a traditional mortgage. Nor is it tethered by the protection of an old-fashioned home loan.

One way to buy a home without a mortgage is to purchase on contract and let the seller provide short-term balloon loan financing at a below-market rate. Balloon loans also are available from traditional mortgage makers, such as mortgage bankers and savings and loan associations. Another way is to assume, or take over, the payments on the seller's mortgage.

When home-loan rates are as high as the ionosphere and mortgage money is as tight as a seat in coach class, financing devices such as contract sales, mortgage assumptions, seller-held balloon loans, and second mortgages soar.

As simple as creative financing sounds, legal experts say that it often may have more inherent risks than tiptoeing on a tightrope without a safety net.

BURSTING BALLOONS

Take a balloon loan, for example. It is attractive because it offers a below-market rate and no closing points—if made by a seller. A lender will charge points at closing, but the rate will be below those on 15-year and 30-year loans. A typical balloon requires a lump-sum payment at the end of a specified term, usually three, five, or seven years. The balloon is said to "pop" at the end of the period.

Consumer advocates warn that home buyers who take off on a home-sale deal funded with a balloon may be floating over tough terrain. If the balloon bursts at an inconvenient time, the buyer could fall into a deep financial chasm.

"What happens when interest rates are higher, not lower, when the balloon comes due?" asks Marshall J. Moltz, a Chicago real estate lawyer. "And, what happens if the buyer's income doesn't increase enough for him to qualify for a conventional loan from a bank or savings and loan?"

If rates are high when the balloon bursts, a buyer's alternatives include getting a conventional mortgage at sky-high rates or renegotiating the balloon at a higher rate. If the balloon is extended by a conventional lender, additional closing points often are charged. If the lender—the seller or conventional lender—won't extend the loan, the homeowner could face foreclosure and could lose the house. And if rates are high, there won't be a squadron of buyers waiting to descend upon your house. If you have to sell, you could end up taking a big loss.

Another depressing thought is that balloons were the predominant form of real estate financing that blew thousands of Americans out of their houses during the 1930s.

In times of high mortgage rates, Moltz said, the only protection for a borrower is writing an automatic extension of the balloon in the contract. For example, specify that the loan be extended 3 years at an interest rate 0.5 percentage point higher than during the original length of the mortgage.

"The seller also has to protect himself in a contract deal," said Moltz. "His lawyer should put a rider into the contract saying that if mortgage rates drop, the buyer has to go out and get a mortgage." That way the seller can take his or her money and be free of the house.

With enough variations of creative financing to fill the basket of a large hot-air balloon, a guide is necessary to help buyers and sellers avoid tripping over a bad deal and tumbling into financial oblivion. Here is a rundown on a few of them:

MORTGAGE ASSUMPTION

Before you buy real estate, ask a seller if his or her mortgage is assumable. It's possible to save thousands of dollars if you can take over a seller's low-rate mortgage and smaller payments.

But don't be lured near a financial canyon without knowing of possible problems that could put you over the edge. For example, a sale based on an assumption could be illegal if the mortgage contains a clause requiring full repayment of the loan if the home is sold. Courts have ruled that, to be effective, a due-on-sale clause must be written into both the mortgage document and the note.

Most due-on-sale mortgages require the loan to be paid off in full if the property is sold on contract, Moltz said. The seller could be slapped with an interest penalty if the lender learns of an illegal contract deal. And the low-rate loan that attracted you to the home will vanish like a mirage, leaving you with payments you can't afford.

One way to avoid due-on-sale provisions is to assume a home loan backed by Uncle Sam. All FHA-insured and VA-guaranteed mortgages are assumable. Also, most conventional mortgages that were taken out 10 or more years ago can be assumed.

The problem with conventional loans that old is that the value of most homes has doubled or tripled since the old mortgage was taken out. Thus, the balance on the mortgage is not nearly enough to cover the financing cost of the house for the new buyer.

That's why so many lending institutions permitted "blended" mortgages during the early 1980s. In return for the seller paying off the low-rate loan, the lender initiated a loan for the buyer at an interest rate above that of the old mortgage but lower than the prevailing market rate.

BALLOON LOANS

The interest rate on balloons made by conventional lenders is usually fixed and always lower than a long-term, fixed-rate mortgage, because the loan is paid off faster. Payments are set up as if you would pay off the loan over 30 years. However, the entire principal amount is due at the end of the specified shorter period.

Maximum loan amounts can vary from $133,250 to $300,000, and down payments run anywhere from 5 percent to 25 percent. Lenders usually charge a $250 closing fee plus closing costs of 2.5 to 3 percent of the loan amount. With a down payment of less than 20 percent, private mortgage insurance is required.

CONTRACT SALES

Most contract sales involve a negotiated down payment and a short-term balloon loan provided by the seller. The loan is like the balloon made by conventional lenders, but it may carry a lower interest rate and no points are charged at closing.

Under the agreement, the seller holds title to the property until the terms of the contract are met. The contract will spell out the amount of down payment, length of contract, and the principal and interest payment to be made by the purchaser.

Although the monthly payments in a contract deal are based on a 25- or 30-year amortization schedule, most contract deals call for a lump-sum balloon payment at a specified time.

Contract buyers do not have the same legal rights as other mortgage borrowers. The biggest risk for a contract buyer is a fast foreclosure triggered by late monthly payments. While it may take as long as a year to foreclose on a mortgage in some states, a contract buyer can be foreclosed on in as little as 60 to 90 days.

If the contract deal is tied to an existing mortgage, problems can arise for the buyer if the seller doesn't meet loan obligations. Experts advise that the buyer's lawyer make provisions in the contract that allow the buyer to pay the lender directly if the seller fails to pay his or her mortgage.

Experts also recommend strongly that the deed be placed in escrow at a title insurance company. This avoids an estate problem if the seller dies before the contract is paid off. Obviously, a real estate lawyer is invaluable for the buyer—and the seller—in a contract sale.

Beware if the property is held in a land trust. In Illinois and other states, if you miss a payment on the contract deal, your beneficial interest in the trust could be sold in as little as 15 days. It's just like missing a payment on an automobile.

PURCHASE-MONEY MORTGAGES

If the owner holds title to the property without a lien and does not need the cash from the sale all at once, he or she can write a mortgage contract and charge the borrower interest. The rate is often far below prevailing interest rates on this seller-held first mortgage because the seller wants to sell the home in a weak housing market.

The biggest difference between this and a contract sale with a balloon is that under a purchase-money mortgage, the buyer gets deed and title to the home at closing.

For unsophisticated sellers, the biggest pitfalls lie in setting the rate too low and in collection risks, Moltz said. "The purchase-money mortgage contract must call for late-payment charges or interest penalties to keep the buyer honest," he recommended.

SELLER-HELD SECOND MORTGAGES

A second mortgage is a loan secured by property that already is secured by a loan—the first mortgage or deed of trust. If the buyer can't obtain a large enough mortgage to purchase a home—or wants to borrow as little as possible at market rates—the seller may extend a second mortgage to make up the difference.

Often this lasts for 1 to 5 years, although the payments on the second mortgage are kept low by figuring them as if the loan would last 25 or 30 years. The balance is due in a balloon payment, or lump sum, at the end of the loan period.

Many lenders, however, won't allow a second mortgage if they learn about it, because they fear this would reduce the borrower's ability to repay the first loan. In an effort to conceal the second mortgage from the primary lender, Moltz said, most seconds are recorded after closing.

Also, the seller holding the second mortgage can be shortchanged if the buyer doesn't make payments on the first mortgage. In case of foreclosure, the holder of the second mortgage would be paid only after the primary lender gets all its money.

BUYDOWNS

A creative financing technique often overlooked by purchasers is provided through mortgage buydowns, or subsidies, from private sellers or builders trying to sell a house quickly. The seller pays a lump sum upfront to the lender who figures this in while setting the monthly payments for the first 2 or 3 years.

Buydowns make the first 2 or 3 years of home ownership financially easier. But remember, there is no free lunch. Usually the cost of the buydown is added to the price of the house. And while mortgages are for 15 or 30 years, buydowns usually run for only 3 years. At the end of the period, the buyer must either obtain new financing and pay off the loan or pay the rate stated in the agreement.

Buydowns may be worth the extra cost if you plan to stay in the home for at least as long as the buydown is in effect. If not, you are paying the full cost of the buydown but not using it.

PREPAYING A MORTGAGE

One of the most creative ways to rapidly pay off a home or at least to build equity quickly is by taking out a 30-year conventional or government-backed mortgage, then prepaying the loan. Every dollar of the prepayment would go to reduce the principal of the loan.

It seldom occurs to homeowners to pay off their mortgage ahead of schedule, because they can't imagine that an extra $50 a month makes much of a difference. But even a small increase in payments that goes exclusively to reduce principal can put thousands of dollars in your pocket over the long term and reduce the length of the mortgage by years.

Tell the bank what you're doing (and be sure that prepayments won't generate a penalty), then include an extra amount in each mortgage check marked "for reduction of principal."

The beauty of prepayment is that you don't have to lock yourself into the larger payments that a shorter-term amortization schedule would require. If you're not sure that you can handle the burden of large monthly payments on a 15-year loan, take the 30-year loan and try to make regular or lump sum prepayments whenever possible. But you are free to choose when an extra payment fits into your budget.

One prepayment rule of thumb is to add to your monthly principal and interest payment an amount equal to the next month's principal payment. You will be given a table outlining each of your 360 monthly payments—and how they are split between principal and interest—when you get a 30-year mortgage.

By making the next month's principal payment in advance, you will be reducing the balance upon which interest is calculated monthly. That means that each future monthly payment—though fixed in amount—will put more toward principal than it would have.

If you follow this procedure regularly, you can save tens of thousands of dollars and cut years off your mortgage.

Though exact calculations of how much this will speed up your loan are complicated, your lender should send you an annual statement detailing how much principal remains. Compare this to the table you received at closing. If at the end of year 2 your principal balance is equal to year 4 on your table, you already have cut 2 years off your mortgage. Your savings in interest would be 24 times your monthly payment.

Before you start, make sure your promissory note does not specifically prohibit prepayment of principal. Some lenders restrict the number of principal prepayments allowed each year. If it is not a violation of the note, you do not need the approval or consent of your lender before you prepay.

It also is important to enclose a note with your mortgage payment informing the lender about the amount of the principal prepayment. For your records, itemize the exact distribution covered in the payment, preferably on the check.

ZERO PERCENT FINANCING

Zero percent financing really may be as good as it sounds. This financing method is rarely seen except when sellers are anxious to make a sale during periods of high interest rates. No financing fees are charged during the one- to five-year term of a zero percent loan. You simply repay the principal rapidly.

One Chicago-area builder, Sundance Homes, used this method to sell suburban homes in 1982, when fixed rates hovered around 15 percent. Buyers were required to make a down payment of at least 33 percent of the purchase price and had 5 years of fixed monthly payments to pay off the rest of the loan. "Today, these buyers own their homes outright, while many of their neighbors still are making hefty principal and interest payments," said Maurice Sanderman, president of Sundance Homes.

Individual sellers also used this method during the early 1980s, but used much shorter terms.

If zero percent financing sounds too good to be true, consider Uncle Sam's position. The federal government allowed buyers who used zero percent financing to consider 10 percent of the principal payment as tax-deductible interest. No one really charges zero percent interest, Uncle Sam says.

That's the first question a borrower should ask: Has the cost of financing been added to the price of the home? In times of unexpectedly weak buyer demand, the financing cost may come from a seller's profit, though perhaps the seller would have cut the price if you had more usual financing.

The second consideration involves cash flow. Because an extraordinarily large down payment is required and the majority of the monthly payment goes to principal, not tax-deductible interest (unlike most mortgage plans), a borrower must have substantial monthly income to handle the payments. After five years, however, the borrower owns the property free and clear.

CHAPTER 18

COMPUTERIZED MORTGAGE HUNTING: THE WAVE OF THE FUTURE

Computerized home-loan hunting is catching on big in Mortgageland. And that can only be good news for borrowers.

Traditionally if a lender wanted to enter a market, he or she would have to hire qualified personnel and set up an office, both costly and time-consuming tasks.

However, lenders from Boston or New York now can offer mortgages to home buyers in Chicago or Topeka, Kansas, without even having hanging out a shingle. This increased competition will force your local financial institution to make interest rates more appealing. And borrowers will reap the benefits.

RENNIE MAE

The latest innovation in Mortgageland is Rennie Mae, a computerized nationwide mortgage system being developed by the National Association of Realtors. The system offers all the types of loans your local lenders do.

"The Rennie Mae network will be available at offices of local Realtors," said John J. Pembroke, president of Dallas-based American Financial Network, which markets the program to brokers on behalf of the association. "And, because it will be open to any lender in the country that wishes to participate, consumers can be given a more complete offering of available mortgages in an unbiased manner."

There are other computerized national mortgage networks. Groups such as Shelternet, LoanExpress, and LoanLink each offer mortgages from a small group of lenders, who jointly market their individual mortgage programs. While they help the consumer by bringing outside competition into the local market, they offer no more variety than a food-store chain that sells only the house brands.

"We're not pushing any favorites," Pembroke said. "We function like a public utility in that we help consumers find the right mortgage for their pocketbook. Unlike a public utility, we don't charge the consumer for our service."

EASY TO USE

The Rennie Mae system is easy to use. To save problems later, buyers can prequalify for a mortgage at a participating Realtor's office. Of course, using Rennie Mae means a buyer must work through a Realtor and not buy a home being sold directly by its owner.

The buyer provides personal financial information required by mortgage lenders. The numbers are fed into a computer, which produces a range of prices that the buyer can afford. The buyer then views mortgages that are sorted by loan type, interest rate, annual percentage rate, and down payment requirements.

For example, if you earn $40,000 a year and have monthly auto loan and credit card debt payments totaling $262, the printout would show that you can qualify for a monthly mortgage principal and interest payment of $833. (As discussed in Chapter 4, you could also figure that 25 percent of your gross monthly income is available for principal and interest payments. In this case, 25 percent of $3,333 per month is $833.) Based on this monthly payment, you should be able to qualify for a 30-year fixed-rate mortgage of $91,100 at an interest rate of 10.5 percent.

However, if lenders are offering mortgages at interest rates of 10 percent, you could qualify for a $94,900 loan. If you choose a 15-year fixed loan at 10 percent you would quality for a loan of only $77,500.

After the consumer reviews all the financing options available, he or she chooses a mortgage and fills out a loan application. Verification forms are entered into the computer and electronically transmitted to the lender. Federal Express is automatically notified to pick up the original signed documents from the real estate office and deliver them to the lender.

"The system allows the lender to immediately begin processing the loan," said Pembroke. "This reduces the time it takes to close the loan."

FINANCED BY LENDERS

The system is financed by the lenders, who pay 0.7 percent of the loan amount for any mortgage originated by the Rennie Mae system. American Financial Network pays the broker a fee of 0.5 percent and pockets 0.2 percent for itself.

The borrower is unaffected because he or she will pay the same origination fees as with any other lender. But the rate may be better, because there is increased competition in every market.

Pembroke said Realtors in the network could run into problems in states such as New Jersey, where a mortgage banking license is required to take a loan application.

CHAPTER 19

TWENTY COMMON QUESTIONS AND ANSWERS ABOUT HOME LOANS

1. How can I figure how much mortgage I can afford?

When lenders figure how much of a loan a home buyer can afford, they use general rules of thumb. They say your mortgage principal and interest payments should not exceed 25 percent of your gross monthly income. When real estate taxes and homeowners' insurance are added, your monthly payments should not exceed 28 percent of your gross income.

Total housing costs plus other long-term debts, such as car payments, student loans, and credit card obligations, should not exceed 33 percent of gross monthly income.

If you can qualify within these guidelines, you should be able to afford a home.

2. Should I take out a mortgage now or wait for rates to go lower?

If you know for certain where rates are going, you should be a millionaire in the bond markets of Wall

Street. In mid-1985, economists sure weren't predicting 9.5 percent fixed-rate loans for early 1986.

In other words, ordinary consumers should grab a rate that makes sense. There's no telling when rates will go up or down. If the financing works out to be a good, affordable deal, take it and be happy. Maybe you won't get the lowest rate of the year, but by waiting for the "perfect" time, you may miss the boat if rates go higher. Also, that home you like today may be sold to someone else tomorrow.

3. Where should I start to look for a mortgage?

Local S&Ls are a good place to start your search for a home loan, because they specialize in long-term mortgages. Also, they tend to be more sensitive to borrowers' needs because they want to service the loan and maintain a good customer relationship. They want to sell their mortgage borrowers their other services, such as savings accounts, home-improvement loans, and certificates of deposit.

However, you may pay a slightly higher rate at an S&L, because most of them handle a lower volume of business than mortgage companies accommodate. And mortgage companies handle only one business: mortgages.

During a strong mortgage market, an S&L may process and approve a loan faster than a mortgage company because the S&L may know the local system better.

4. Because lenders seem to be so competitive, aren't all their rates about the same?

No. Like supermarkets and department stores, lending institutions have different costs and desired profit margins. Also, they try to establish different client bases. Consequently, lenders' offerings can differ in rates, points, and fees.

5. How many lenders should I call for loan-rate quotes when shopping for a mortgage?

An old rule of thumb was three. That was true in the days of homogeneous lenders and mortgages. In the deregulated and highly competitive market that exists now, three probably is too few.

Why not get out your local phone book and phone every lender in there? Sure, this will take a little bit of time. But consider that every $10 in monthly payments means 180 or 360 months at $10. That's $1,800 to $3,600 over the course of a 15-year loan and a 30-year loan, respectively. So, calling lots of lenders may be a very good investment.

6. How much will it cost to take out a mortgage?

That depends on the lender, but figure on paying about 4.5 percent of the home's costs in points and fees. When you compare loans from different lenders, look at all costs, not just rates and points.

When you talk to a potential lender, ask which of the following fees apply to loans: points, title search, title exam insurance, application fee, credit report, real estate lawyer fees, appraisal fee, loan origination fee, recording taxes, and private mortgage insurance.

When you close, you also will have to prepay the first year's homeowners' insurance premium and pro-rated property taxes. Ask your realty agent if the seller will pay any of these fees. Also ask if there are any other fees the lender charges.

7. Is it a good idea to lock in the interest rate that is in effect when I make my loan application? Is there a fee for this?

Ask exactly when the rate you are applying for will be established. With rates fluctuating daily, a homeowner should determine whether the rate will be the one available on the day of the application or the one available on the day of the closing. If a lender will give you the rate quoted at application time for no additional fee, you probably would be wise to take it.

Some lenders, however, charge up to a full point extra at application time if a homeowner wants to be locked in to a chosen rate if closing is within a specified period of time. If rates move lower, this money would be wasted. Sometimes, locking in the rate doesn't pay even if rates move higher. In 1986, thousands of borrowers who paid for a locked rate still got burned because of mortgage processing delays. Sixty-day rate commitments expired, and borrowers had to pay current market rates, which happened to be higher than at application time.

Other times, however, locking in pays off handsomely. One home buyer in the western suburbs of Chicago applied for a 30-year fixed-rate loan in May 1986. The lender guaranteed the rate for 60 days with no fee. Because the buyer had to take time to sell his town house, he paid 0.5 percent of the loan amount in points to lock in the 10-percent rate for an extra 30 days. By the time he closed in August, rates had climbed to 10.5 percent. Locking in paid off.

8. Should I choose a fixed-rate loan or an adjustable-rate mortgage?

That question cannot be answered simply. If you intend to stay in your home for just a few years, chances are the adjustable-rate mortgage will cost you less. The first-year rate probably will be at least 2 percentage points lower than for a fixed-rate loan, because lenders want to attract ARM business. In the second year, the ARM rate probably will increase to about the level of the fixed-rate loan. The lower rate in the first year makes the ARM a short-term bargain.

However, if you intend to stay in the home for at least several years, there are different considerations. If you don't mind the risk of fluctuating rates and your budget can absorb payment increases, you may want to stick with the ARM and see where rates go. Or you may prefer the peace of mind of a fixed-rate loan; over the long haul, the ARM could go several points higher—or lower—than the fixed.

Without a crystal ball, it's impossible to tell where rates will be a few years from now. With a fixed-rate loan, you know what you'll be paying each and every month for a very long time. With an ARM, you know only the maximum and perhaps the minimum rates you'll be paying—and the maximum is much higher than the current fixed rates.

9. What's better—a 15-year mortgage or a 30-year loan?

More and more home buyers are considering 15-year loans because today's lower rates make the higher payments affordable. The interest savings are dramatic with a 15-year loan. And it's amazing how much faster equity is built up in a 15-year loan. That equity is helpful if you are planning to move up to a larger home or just want to be done making mortgage payments. Also, lenders usually charge a slightly lower rate on a 15-year loan than on a 30-year mortgage.

This example may make the difference clearer: On a $50,000 loan at 10 percent for 15 years, you would owe $40,650 after five years. Had you chosen a 30-year loan at 10 percent, you would owe $48,300 after five years.

The difference is even more dramatic after 15 years. You have paid off that 15-year loan, but you'd still owe $40,850 on the 30-year mortgage.

However, if you can't afford the higher payments of a 15-year mortgage, a 30-year loan will give you the advantage of higher federal income-tax deductions for mortgage interest.

10. I just finished law school and landed a well-paying job. But I have very little money to put down on a home. Also, I have lots of school loans to pay off in the next few years. Am I out of luck on a home until then?

Not necessarily. Graduated-payment mortgages were designed for people just like you. The payments start out relatively low, but increase annually for a specified period. This allows you to have a home and get on your feet financially. There are substantial tax benefits in the early years of the loan that will help you every April 15.

As your payments increase, you start to really build up equity. This equity will be helpful in buying a bigger home down the road. One word of caution: If you can, avoid graduated-payment mortgages that feature negative amortization, or you can end up owing more than you did at the beginning of the loan.

11. Will my mortgage payment be more expensive if I can't come up with a 20 percent down payment?

If your down payment is less than 20 percent, you will be required to pay a private mortgage insurance premium. PMI should not be confused with life insurance; PMI paid by the borrower merely protects the lender.

With a 10-percent down payment, you would have to pay 0.5 percent of the mortgage amount at closing to cover the first year's premium. On a $90,000 mortgage, that's $450.

The second year's PMI with a 10-percent down payment will be 0.34 percent of the loan balance. On the $90,000 loan, it would be about $300—paid in 12 monthly installments of about $25.

PMI payments usually continue until you have paid off enough of the mortgage to reach 20 percent of the purchase price.

12. Why do I have to pay points and fees when taking out a mortgage?

Lenders say borrowers have to pay the freight of

originating the loan. Mortgage fees, like the price of a new car, are negotiable. They tend to be substantially higher than the actual cost of doing the work because lenders charge what the market will bear. When rates are low and borrowing activity is high, some lenders cash in. So, shop around.

13. Am I better off paying more points at closing to get a lower rate on the loan?

First, you should realize that the long-run difference between the choices is not all that substantial. Otherwise, the lender would not be so willing to offer more than one choice.

By paying more points, however, you are tying up more of your money upfront. If you move within two or three years, those upfront costs are gone. But if you prefer to have a smaller monthly obligation and expect to stay for more than five years, go ahead and pay the points.

14. How long will it take to close on a mortgage from the time I make the application?

It's impossible to say how long this will take, but be prepared for a wait. Once you begin the process, however, you usually can lock in a rate with the lender.

There are a number of things you can do to speed up the process. These include paying the loan application fee immediately, alerting your employer that an employment verification is on the way, getting copies of your tax forms for the last two years, providing the lender with account number and address for bank and stock accounts and credit cards. Also, you should provide the lender with names and addresses on all loans you have paid off.

15. Do I need an attorney to handle the closing of my home?

You are entering a contract that will obligate you to repay perhaps hundreds of thousands of dollars. You should have an attorney involved in such a substantial undertaking.

16. Do I need to hire a home inspector to check over the property before I buy it?

It is an excellent idea for the buyer of a home to hire an independent engineer or home inspector to check the property for termites and potential structural and mechanical defects. The inspector also will note small matters such as low water pressure and cracked window panes. This usually costs $250. Attach a rider to the sales contract making purchase contingent upon the inspector's approval.

17. We are a retired couple with grown children. We don't want to sell our home, which is paid off. How can we tap our home's equity to meet expenses?

One possibility is a Grannie Mae mortgage. It involves selling your home to your children, then renting it back from them at fair market value under a lifetime lease. The proceeds are invested, and you receive a monthly income check for the rest of your lives. The rent payment is given to your children, who pay the mortgage.

18. My husband and I have saved only a few thousand dollars. How can we buy a home?

If you have a steady job and earn enough to qualify for a Federal Housing Administration–insured mortgage you can buy a $60,000 home with a down payment of as little as $2,500. You also will have to pay a loan origination fee of 1 percent of the loan amount, plus another 1 percent for closing costs—a total of $1,150. In addition, there may be discount points, which you may split with the seller.

19. I'm a World War II veteran who bought a home under the GI Bill and paid it off. Can I buy another home with a VA loan?

Veterans whose previous loans have been paid in full are eligible for new loans guaranteed by the Veterans Administration. If a veteran sells a home purchased with a VA mortgage, he or she can get another VA loan once the first is paid off.

By the way, because you must be nearing retirement (having served more than 40 years ago), you might want to consider a VA loan with a length of less than 30 years. Also, compare conventional loans with VA loans before deciding.

20. We are interested in buying a home but can't qualify for a mortgage. What are the dangers of buying on contract?

Contract buyers do not have the same legal rights as other mortgage borrowers. In particular, late monthly payments can trigger a fast foreclosure. While it may take as long as a year to foreclose on a mortgage, a contract buyer can be foreclosed on in as little as 60 to 90 days.

Another problem is that sellers rarely even consider a contract sale except during weak housing markets. You may have a hard time finding someone who doesn't want all the money immediately.

A final point: A lender isn't disqualifying you for a loan because he or she doesn't like you. Over time, lenders learn that buyers with insufficient income frequently are foreclosed on. Make sure you have enough income to cover your home purchase, or you could end up losing everything you put into a house—and ruin your credit history, too.

LOAN AMORTIZATION AND LOAN PROGRESS TABLES

HOW TO USE
LOAN AMORTIZATION TABLES

Every mortgage borrower should know how to use a loan amortization table. Once you know current interest rates, it's easy to figure out what mortgage payment it will take to pay off a loan over 15 or 30 years.

This is how lenders do it: Look across from the interest rate and down from the mortgage amount. Where they intersect is the monthly payment for principal and interest. For example, the monthly principal and interest for a 30-year loan at 10 percent for $60,000 would be $526.55.

If your mortgage amount is not one of those listed, this procedure is just a little bit harder. Look across from the interest rate to the cost for a $1,000 loan. Then multiply that number by the amount of your loan in thousands. For example, a 30-year loan at 10 percent would cost $8.78 per $1,000. For a $66,000 loan, it would cost $8.78 times 66, or $579.48.

Monthly Payments to Amortize
30-Year Fixed-Rate Loan

Interest Rate	Mortgage Amount					
	$1,000	$40,000	$50,000	$60,000	$70,000	$100,000
8.00%	$7.34	$293.51	$366.89	$440.26	$513.64	$733.77
8.25	7.52	300.51	375.64	450.76	525.89	751.27
8.50	7.69	307.57	384.46	461.35	538.24	768.92
8.75	7.87	314.69	393.36	472.03	550.70	786.71
9.00	8.05	321.85	402.32	482.78	563.24	804.63
9.25	8.23	329.08	411.34	493.61	575.88	822.68
9.50	8.41	336.35	420.43	504.52	588.60	840.86
9.75	8.60	343.67	429.58	515.50	601.41	854.16
10.00	8.78	351.03	438.79	526.55	614.31	877.58
10.25	8.97	358.45	448.06	537.67	627.28	896.11
10.50	9.15	365.90	457.37	548.85	640.32	914.74
10.75	9.34	373.40	466.75	560.09	653.44	933.49
11.00	9.53	380.93	476.17	571.40	666.63	952.33
11.25	9.72	388.51	485.64	582.76	679.89	971.27
11.50	9.91	396.12	495.15	594.18	693.21	990.30
11.75	10.10	403.77	504.71	605.65	706.59	1,009.41
12.00	10.29	411.45	514.31	617.17	720.03	1,028.62
12.50	10.68	426.91	533.63	640.36	747.09	1,067.26
13.00	11.07	442.48	553.10	663.72	774.34	1,106.20
13.50	11.46	458.17	572.71	687.25	801.79	1,145.42
14.00	11.85	473.95	592.44	710.93	829.42	1,184.88
14.50	12.25	489.83	612.28	734.74	857.19	1,224.56
15.00	12.65	505.78	632.23	758.67	885.12	1,264.45

Monthly Payments to Amortize
15-Year Fixed-Rate Loan

Interest Rate	\$1,000	\$40,000	\$50,000	\$60,000	\$70,000	\$100,000
			Mortgage Amount			
8.00%	\$9.56	\$382.27	\$477.83	\$573.40	\$668.96	\$955.66
8.25	9.71	388.06	485.08	582.09	679.10	970.15
8.50	9.85	393.90	492.37	590.85	689.32	984.74
8.75	10.00	399.78	499.73	599.67	699.62	999.45
9.00	10.15	405.71	507.14	608.56	709.99	1,014.27
9.25	10.30	411.68	514.60	617.52	720.44	1,029.20
9.50	10.45	417.69	522.12	626.54	730.96	1,044.23
9.75	10.60	423.75	529.69	635.62	741.56	1,059.37
10.00	10.75	429.85	537.31	644.77	752.23	1,074.61
10.25	10.90	435.99	544.98	653.98	762.97	1,089.96
10.50	11.06	442.16	552.70	663.24	773.78	1,105.40
10.75	11.21	448.38	560.48	672.57	784.67	1,120.95
11.00	11.37	454.64	568.30	681.96	795.62	1,136.60
11.25	11.53	460.94	576.18	691.41	806.65	1,152.35
11.50	11.69	467.28	584.10	700.92	817.74	1,168.19
11.75	11.85	473.66	592.07	710.48	828.90	1,184.14
12.00	12.01	480.07	600.09	720.11	840.12	1,200.17
12.50	12.33	493.01	616.27	739.52	862.77	1,232.53
13.00	12.66	506.10	632.63	759.15	885.67	1,265.25
13.50	12.99	519.33	649.16	779.00	908.83	1,298.32
14.00	13.32	532.70	665.88	799.05	932.22	1,331.75
14.50	13.66	546.21	682.76	819.31	955.86	1,365.51
15.00	14.00	559.84	699.80	839.76	979.72	1,399.59

HOW TO USE
LOAN PROGRESS TABLES

Loan progress tables will help you know how much of your loan will be paid off after set amounts of time have elapsed.

First, find the interest rate of your loan in the left column. Next, in the second column, find the original term—or length—of your loan. Then run your finger across to the year of the loan that you are interested in. The figure represents the amount of principal remaining to be paid off for each $1,000 of your loan. To find the total remaining principal, multiply this number by the amount of your loan in thousands.

For example, after 5 years of a 30-year loan at 10 percent, you would still owe $966 of each $1,000 you borrowed. On a $60,000 loan, you would still owe $966 times 60, or $57,960.

After 20 years on that same 10-percent, 30-year loan, you would still owe $664 of each $1,000 originally borrowed. On that $60,000 loan, you would still owe $664 times 60, or $39,840.

Loan Progress Table

Showing the dollar balance remaining per $1,000 of loan

Interest Rate	Original Term	Elapsed Term in Years									
		2	5	8	10	12	15	18	20	22	25
8⅛%	10	859	600	269							
	15	926	789	615	473	307					
	20	957	877	775	692	595	415	186			
	25	973	924	861	810	750	639	499	384	248	
	30	983	952	912	879	841	771	682	609	523	365
8¼%	10	860	601	271							
	15	927	791	617	476	308					
	20	957	878	777	695	597	418	188			
	25	974	925	863	813	753	643	502	387	251	
	30	983	953	914	882	844	774	685	613	527	368
8⅜%	10	861	603	272							
	15	927	793	620	478	310					
	20	958	880	780	697	600	420	189			
	25	974	927	865	815	756	646	505	390	253	
	30	984	954	915	884	847	778	689	616	530	372
8½%	10	861	604	273							
	15	928	794	622	480	312					
	20	958	881	782	700	603	423	191			
	25	975	928	867	818	759	649	508	392	255	
	30	984	955	917	886	849	781	693	620	534	375
8⅝%	10	862	606	274							
	15	929	796	624	482	314					
	20	959	883	784	703	606	426	192			
	25	975	929	869	820	762	653	512	395	257	
	30	985	956	919	888	852	784	696	624	538	378
8¾%	10	863	607	275							
	15	929	797	626	484	315					
	20	960	884	786	705	609	428	194			
	25	976	930	871	823	765	656	515	398	259	
	30	985	957	920	890	854	787	700	628	542	381
8⅞%	10	864	609	276							
	15	930	799	628	486	317					
	20	960	886	788	708	611	431	195			
	25	976	932	873	825	767	659	518	401	262	
	30	985	958	922	892	857	790	703	631	546	384
9%	10	865	610	277							
	15	931	801	630	489	319					
	20	961	887	791	710	614	433	197			
	25	977	933	875	827	770	662	522	404	264	
	30	986	959	924	894	859	793	707	635	549	388
9⅛%	10	865	612	278							
	15	931	802	633	491	321					
	20	961	888	793	713	617	436	198			
	25	977	934	877	830	773	666	525	407	266	
	30	986	960	925	896	862	796	711	639	553	391
9¼%	10	866	613	280							
	15	932	804	635	493	322					
	20	962	890	795	715	620	439	200			
	25	978	935	879	832	776	669	528	410	268	
	30	986	961	927	898	864	799	714	643	557	394
9⅜%	10	867	615	281							
	15	933	805	637	495	324					
	20	962	891	797	718	622	441	201			
	25	978	936	881	834	778	672	531	413	271	
	30	987	962	928	900	866	802	717	646	560	397

Loan Progress Table

Showing the dollar balance remaining per $1,000 of loan

Interest Rate	Original Term	Elapsed Term in Years									
		2	5	8	10	12	15	18	20	22	25
9½%	10	868	616	282							
	15	934	807	639	497	326					
	20	963	893	799	720	625	444	203			
	25	978	937	883	837	781	675	535	416	273	
	30	987	962	930	902	869	805	721	650	564	400
9⅝%	10	869	618	283							
	15	934	809	641	499	328					
	20	964	894	801	723	628	446	205			
	25	979	938	885	839	784	678	538	419	275	
	30	987	963	931	904	871	808	724	653	568	404
9¾%	10	869	619	284							
	15	935	810	643	501	330					
	20	964	895	803	725	631	449	206			
	25	979	940	886	841	786	681	541	422	277	
	30	988	964	933	906	873	811	728	657	571	407
9⅞%	10	870	621	285							
	15	936	812	645	504	331					
	20	965	897	805	728	633	452	208			
	25	980	941	888	843	789	685	544	425	279	
	30	988	965	934	908	876	814	731	661	575	410
10%	10	871	622	286							
	15	936	813	647	506	333					
	20	965	898	807	730	636	454	209			
	25	980	942	890	846	792	688	547	428	282	
	30	988	966	935	909	878	817	734	664	578	413
10⅛%	10	872	623	288							
	15	937	815	649	508	335					
	20	966	899	810	733	639	457	211			
	25	980	943	892	848	794	691	551	431	284	
	30	989	967	937	911	880	819	738	668	582	416
10¼%	10	872	625	289							
	15	937	816	651	510	337					
	20	966	901	812	735	641	459	212			
	25	981	944	893	850	797	694	554	433	286	
	30	989	967	938	913	882	822	741	671	585	419
10⅜%	10	873	626	290							
	15	938	818	654	512	338					
	20	967	902	814	738	644	462	214			
	25	981	945	895	852	799	697	557	436	288	
	30	989	968	939	915	884	825	744	674	589	422
10½%	10	874	628	291							
	15	939	819	656	514	340					
	20	967	903	816	740	647	464	215			
	25	982	946	897	854	802	700	560	439	290	
	30	989	969	941	916	886	828	747	678	592	426
10⅝%	10	875	629	292							
	15	939	821	658	516	342					
	20	968	904	818	742	649	467	217			
	25	982	947	898	856	804	703	563	442	293	
	30	990	970	942	918	888	830	750	681	596	429
10¾%	10	875	631	293							
	15	940	822	660	519	344					
	20	968	906	820	745	652	470	218			
	25	982	948	900	858	807	706	566	445	295	
	30	990	970	943	919	890	833	754	685	599	432

Loan Progress Table

Showing the dollar balance remaining per $1,000 of loan

Interest Rate	Original Term	2	5	8	10	12	15	18	20	22	25
					Elapsed Term in Years						
10⅞%	10	876	632	294							
	15	941	824	662	521	345					
	20	969	907	821	747	654	472	220			
	25	983	949	901	860	809	709	569	448	297	
	30	990	971	944	921	892	835	757	688	603	435
11%	10	877	634	296							
	15	941	825	664	523	347					
	20	969	908	823	749	657	475	221			
	25	983	950	903	862	812	712	572	451	299	
	30	990	972	945	923	894	838	760	691	606	438
11⅛%	10	878	635	297							
	15	942	827	666	525	349					
	20	970	909	825	752	660	477	223			
	25	983	950	905	864	814	714	575	454	302	
	30	991	972	947	924	896	840	763	695	610	441
11¼%	10	878	636	298							
	15	942	828	668	527	351					
	20	970	911	827	754	662	480	225			
	25	984	951	906	866	816	717	579	456	304	
	30	991	973	948	926	898	843	766	698	613	444
11⅜%	10	879	638	299							
	15	943	829	670	529	352					
	20	971	912	829	756	665	482	226			
	25	984	952	908	868	819	720	582	459	306	
	30	991	974	949	927	900	845	769	701	616	447
11½%	10	880	639	300							
	15	944	831	672	531	354					
	20	971	913	831	759	667	485	228			
	25	984	953	909	870	821	723	585	462	308	
	30	991	974	950	929	902	848	772	704	620	450
11⅝%	10	881	641	301							
	15	944	832	674	533	356					
	20	971	914	833	761	670	487	229			
	25	985	954	911	872	823	726	588	465	310	
	30	992	975	951	930	903	850	775	708	623	453
11¾%	10	881	642	302							
	15	945	834	676	535	358					
	20	972	915	835	763	672	490	231			
	25	985	955	912	874	826	729	591	468	313	
	30	992	975	952	931	905	852	777	711	626	456
11⅞%	10	882	644	304							
	15	945	835	678	537	360					
	20	972	916	837	765	675	492	232			
	25	985	956	913	876	828	731	594	471	315	
	30	992	976	953	933	907	855	780	714	630	459
12%	10	883	645	305							
	15	946	837	680	540	361					
	20	973	917	838	767	677	495	234			
	25	986	957	915	878	830	734	597	473	317	
	30	992	977	954	934	909	857	783	717	633	462
12⅛%	10	884	648	307							
	15	947	839	684	544	365					
	20	974	920	842	772	682	500	237			
	25	986	958	918	881	835	740	603	479	322	
	30	993	978	956	937	912	862	789	723	639	468

Loan Progress Table

Showing the dollar balance remaining per $1,000 of loan

Interest Rate	Original Term	Elapsed Term in Years									
		2	5	8	10	12	15	18	20	22	25
12½%	10	886	651	309							
	15	948	842	688	548	368					
	20	974	922	845	776	687	505	240			
	25	987	960	920	885	839	745	608	485	326	
	30	993	979	958	939	915	866	794	729	646	474
12¾%	10	887	653	312							
	15	949	845	692	552	372					
	20	975	924	849	780	692	510	243			
	25	987	961	923	888	843	750	614	490	330	
	30	993	980	960	942	918	870	800	735	652	480
13%	10	888	656	314							
	15	950	847	695	556	376					
	20	976	926	852	785	697	515	246			
	25	988	963	926	891	847	755	620	496	335	
	30	994	981	962	944	922	874	805	741	658	486
13¼%	10	890	659	316							
	15	952	850	699	560	379					
	20	977	928	856	789	702	520	250			
	25	988	964	928	895	851	760	626	501	339	
	30	994	982	963	946	924	878	810	747	664	492
13½%	10	891	662	319							
	15	953	853	703	564	383					
	20	977	930	859	793	707	525	253			
	25	989	965	930	898	855	765	631	507	343	
	30	994	983	965	949	927	882	815	752	670	498
13¾%	10	892	665	321							
	15	954	855	707	568	386					
	20	978	932	862	797	711	530	256			
	25	989	967	933	901	859	770	637	512	348	
	30	995	983	967	951	930	886	820	758	676	504
14%	10	894	667	323							
	15	955	858	711	572	390					
	20	979	934	865	801	716	534	259			
	25	990	968	935	904	863	775	642	517	352	
	30	995	984	968	953	933	890	824	763	682	509
14¼%	10	895	670	326							
	15	956	860	714	576	393					
	20	980	936	868	805	720	539	262			
	25	990	969	937	907	867	780	648	523	357	
	30	995	985	970	955	935	893	829	768	688	515
14½%	10	896	673	328							
	15	957	863	718	580	397					
	20	980	937	871	809	725	544	265			
	25	991	970	939	910	870	785	653	528	361	
	30	996	986	971	957	938	897	834	774	694	520
14¾%	10	898	675	330							
	15	957	865	722	584	400					
	20	981	939	874	812	729	549	268			
	25	991	972	941	912	874	789	658	533	365	
	30	996	987	972	959	940	900	838	779	699	526
15%	10	899	678	333							
	15	958	868	725	588	404					
	20	981	941	877	816	734	554	272			
	25	991	973	943	915	877	794	664	538	369	
	30	996	987	973	960	942	903	842	784	705	532

ABOUT
THE AUTHOR
AND EDITOR

Author Don DeBat, an award-winning real estate editor, has covered the mortgage, finance, and housing markets for nearly two decades. He is widely known for his consumer-oriented columns that appear in the *Chicago Sun-Times.*

In 1983 DeBat's story "The Mortgage Race" won first place in the consumer category of the National Association of Real Estate Editors writing contest. The article outlined 12 ways to finance the purchase of a home.

In 1982 "The ARMs Race" pointed out the drawbacks of financing a home with an adjustable-rate mortgage, and "The Perils of Creative Finance " delved into the pitfalls of buying a home on contract with short-term balloon financing. The articles won national citations from the Real Estate Educators Association and the National Association of Real Estate Editors.

A real estate investor, DeBat has renovated and

restored two vintage homes in Chicago, and he once headed a community group that won historic landmark district status for a city neighborhood. DeBat received his master's degree in 1968 and a bachelor's degree in 1966 from the University of Missouri School of Journalism in Columbia.

Editor Thomas A. Kelly holds a master of management degree from Northwestern University's Kellogg Graduate School of Management with concentrations in finance and marketing.

His financial expertise contributed to a *Chicago Sun-Times* series inspecting private mortgage insurance. The series was first runner-up in the 1985 National Association of Real Estate Editors contest and won the 1986 feature reporting award from the Financial Institutions Marketing Association.

Kelly, who also holds a bachelor of science degree from Northwestern's Medill School of Journalism, is chief of the *Sun-Times* features copy desk.

INDEX